LOVING DANGEROUSLY:
Journey to Nepal

A True Story of Adventure and Risk

By Lynda Cain Hubbard

HUGO HOUSE PUBLISHERS, LTD.

ISBN: 978-1-936449-61-3

Library of Congress Control Number: 2014945318

Cover Painting: Lynda Cain Hubbard

Cover Design and Interior Formatting: Taylor by Design

Cover Photo: Ronda Taylor

Disclaimer: The events recounted are true; some of the names have been changed. The purpose of this book is to entertain. The author and/or publisher do not guarantee that anyone following these techniques, suggestions, tips, ideas, or strategies will become successful. The author and/or publisher shall have neither liability nor responsibility to anyone with respect to any loss or damage caused, or alleged to be caused, directly or indirectly by the information contained in this book.

Hugo House Publishers, Ltd.
Denver, Colorado
Austin, Texas
www.HugoHousePublishers.com

Contents

Dedication

This book is dedicated to Layla Ellen Richeson, seen here at one month old, and her wonderful mother, Anjuli Hubbard Richeson, as well as all those bright souls who pass along their own wisdom from father to son, mother to daughter, grandparent to grandchild, in every generation...

Preface

LOOKING DOWN AT YOUR BEAUTIFUL, BABY-BLUE EYES SHINING UP AT ME *reminds me of my duty. I have a duty to you, my little one, to tell you the real story of what happened. People make mistakes, and I'm not pulling any punches here so you know whether it is a mom, dad, or grandma, we are not perfect. It is also my duty to pass along a little magic and adventure that greatly influenced my own life and made me more aware of my goofs, but more importantly how to finally overcome them. We all have our own journey of discovery, if open to it, and you will as well. Take what you need from it.*

I have written this especially for you, my dearest granddaughter, when you are ready. This is a true story of how I went from innocence to awareness and the hard-won lessons I learned in retrospect. You will face your own situations and have to deal with them yourself. Maybe, just maybe, my story will give you the added insight to step back, take a good look and see what's really there and learn who you are, who you want to be, as well as what you really want to do.

It started when I was first aware that I was studying life when I studied art. I remember sitting on my own grandmother's lap when I was three years old, drawing on a sketchpad.

The world, I observed intently. To be able to draw it made it an even more wondrous place. I thought people could see what I saw, think what I thought, and therefore lived happy, joyful lives like me, forever curious about the things around me. This was my blissful world and like most children I wanted everyone else to be happy too. It hurt me to think I couldn't make them see or be exuberant about life and took it upon myself as a kind of blame if they weren't. *Why couldn't I make them happy?*

When I was five or six, however, my dad and a few relatives told me I asked way too many questions. They acted annoyed, like it was wrong to be too curious or too excited about things. That stumped me, causing the first gap between me and others. I had to wonder: *What are they seeing? Don't they view that beautiful sunset over there as a wonder? See that light in the air making all those colors? When people grow up, does that mean they stop looking or seeing? Does it mean I will lose how I see things, too, when a grown up? Oh, no!*

But I went on creating moments of pleasure, laughing whenever and wherever I could and being sad if I couldn't. Even though I wasn't supposed to ask questions, fortunately I was still young enough that no one called me "crazy" for using my imagination. I truly believed in the *Little Engine That Could,* who always said, "I think I can, I think I can, I think I can"… until he did it. I thought I was that little engine. But as I got older I ran into some things I couldn't handle myself and had to seek help. Thanks to my own grandparents, I had a refuge. Whenever things went wrong, I thought, "*Nothing can harm me up at the lake.*"

I look back to the time I was a child, Layla, and see the image of our family's log cabin with pine trees surrounding it and the cool blue waters reflecting sunshine upon three little girls on the dock. It's me with two of my ten-year-old friends lying down on towels, all stretched out in a row side by side! Soaking up the sun with our eyes closed, we are whispering about how the clouds look like animals or people, whispering about our families, whispering about our hopes and dreams of being a dancer or a singer. Also we're laughing and describing our brothers acting lame over a pretty girl. Then we each silently pray we can remain like this forever.

Suddenly the flow of bodies turns over as if in a ballet. We all decide at the same time we've had enough sun shining on our faces, so hot and pink. We are Princesses of the Lake. We are magical and the world is ours.

Finally we all give a luxurious stretch, thinking as one, and someone gives a lazy comment about going to the trading post that finally inspires us to rise up. As we lift our tanned, young bodies off the dock, the spell is broken and we all talk at once. The simplicity and peace I find there keeps me grounded, no matter what happens.

As an older child, the adults I often questioned seemed to think it was more polite for children to be quiet, yet they praised my ability to draw and paint with verve. One of my aunts, Aunt Agnes, who was also known for her drinking at family gatherings, caught me on the stairs one time and said, "Your talent, Lynda, is a gift from God."

"Oh, uh, really?… I mean, thank you," I said a little embarrassed.

"Don't thank me, thank God!" she said firmly, and then gave me a wink.

Then at about age fifteen, I realized I was the only artist in our circle of friends and family and everyone else was busy thinking about "making money" or going on vacation in the summer. As I got older, I traveled through the national parks across the U.S. Whenever I did, I took my sketch pad and paints, drawing portraits of the tourists in the park. This is what gave me objectivity, and I saw things from a distance as well as close up, studying people and objects in-depth in order to draw or paint them accurately. I even made twenty-five bucks a picture and came back after that summer with a stash of cash. Showing it to my mom and dad, I told them, "Look, you can't say an artist or someone doing what they love can't make any money!" My mom laughed and my dad nodded, and later they helped me get into Minneapolis Art College. I contributed, taking jobs during the school year and painted during summers whenever I could, earning my keep.

More and more, I realized people did not see life as I did and didn't think like I did. This always surprised and disappointed me, like I was really from another galaxy and just happened to end up on Earth. But, perhaps even more, I wanted to figure out exactly what others *did* think. I made it a game to gain some understanding of people, their emotions, motivations and reactions. I needed to know why some people think only of negative things. I vowed to never give up my own view of life and always keep a sense of humor, if I could. *Thinking back to the best times, with family playing games around a huge table on the porch up at the lake, laughter was a kind of therapy that dissolved differences and something everyone could easily relate to.*

The one thing I knew with certainty was that I needed a lot more information, more experience. That led me to the first and perhaps the most powerful journey of my life: to Nepal and back.

Introduction

Y OU HAVE TO REMEMBER, LAYLA, THIS WAS A TURBULENT TIME—JUST after the sixties, not yet the eighties, supercharged with sex, full of drugs and rock and roll that had not yet mellowed out into disco. One president, Nixon, left office in disgrace, while his successor ended an un-winnable war in Vietnam—a place far away few had studied, let alone cared about. Things were still a bit rocky politically but on their way to stabilizing out.

It seemed to be a good time to travel, since Americans were still welcomed and admired in most countries, even envied. The dollar was strong and our men were cocky. The Women's Rights movement was potent, opening up work and sexual opportunities that had been frowned upon earlier. But the experience of the "free love" sixties had lost some of its luster. Women were more careful as well as more selective. But there was still enough wildness in the air. This was the seventies, and I was smack in the middle of it!

Chapter One

Riding on Top

M Y FIRST GLIMPSE OF NEPAL WAS FROM AN ANCIENT BUS. CATCHING IT IN INDIA, just before the Nepal border, I was riding on the top with a perfect view. No way was I going to squeeze inside among the noisy Nepalese jammed like cat food in a rusty can. So I did the next best thing.

I asked in my most sincere but flirty voice, "I want to ride on top of the bus, on the backpacks, please?" Presenting the driver with a few rupees (the Nepalese currency) at the same time, he gave a nod, took the money and agreed.

With a twinkle in his eye, he said, "Anything for you, little one.. I was twenty and looked younger. He was a much older man, dressed in traditional shabby cotton shorts and vest with a small Nepalese cloth hat. *But a bit of chivalry and humor in all this chaos I could appreciate. Also I learned that greasing the wheels with a little cash was much more effective than complaining!*

Riding on the top of the bus sitting on backpacks, I had a clear view of terraced rice paddies and people, in colorful cotton shifts or tattered cotton shorts and vests, bending over to cultivate the rice crops as we drove along. Then, looking up, I suddenly saw the Himalayas rising above them, framing the scene like a picture with green hills lazily rolling down to the rice paddies. Over to the left, I spotted the most eclectic city I had ever seen. *You may think of the most exotic science fiction movies, Layla, yet here it was in front of me.* The panorama spread out before me like an exotic quilt of raw earth stitched with green shoots of rice between the jewel-colored splotches of the workers' clothing, all in a terraced pattern before me. As the bus turned through the mountain pass, we entered another world—the world of Kathmandu Valley in the Kingdom of Nepal.

Then it hit me. *I'm really here!* No concrete. No freeways full of cars or tall steel and glass buildings like at home. Just rice paddies with emerald-colored shoots hung with drops of water sparkling in long rows terraced all the way up the giant hills, surrounded by the twenty-six-thousand-feet-high Himalayas. *Were the mountains floating ABOVE the clouds?* The variety of structures and the riot of colorful reds, blues, browns, and pastels from the clothing of the people shocked my senses into overdrive. I was on full alert and colors seized my attention.

One of the first things I noticed—the air and light was different in Nepal. A golden-warmth suffused the landscape, bringing out the green color of new rice sprouts in detail and the deep purples and stone grey of the mighty snow-topped mountain ranges against a cerulean sky.

I'd been sketching all along my travels and tried to translate what I saw onto paper as much as possible. People were interacting, moving, but with a sense of cohesiveness like they knew where they were going and taking their time. I caught myself studying those around me, which I did when I wanted to paint them. *In some ways, I could discern what they were thinking, or feeling, by looking at them.* The eyes of the Nepalese were big and expressive. They were almond-shaped, brown or sometimes hazel, but not slanted like the Chinese. The Hindu married women had red painted dots on their foreheads right about where the third eye is supposed to be. Women dressed in long skirts of woven cotton in many colors or plain with peasant blouses or tight-fitting faded cotton tops with eyes set off by their copper-brown skin and jet-black hair. Nepalese men wore long white cotton pants and loose shirts or cotton shorts and vests, with their country's small hat (the "nori"). The Tibetan monks walked along slowly with long, deep burgundy or yellow saffron robes, depending upon their status. Indian "gurus" sat cross legged in front of small Hindu temples throughout the city, all in white cotton with scraggly long grey hair and beards. Their eyes looked stoned. Europeans were in jeans or comfortable pants and shirts, both male and female, with solid hiking boots or sandals. They all seemed to dress like back-packers, except those very few in business attire. The palette of people I saw around me screamed to be painted, so I began sketching to try and capture this glorious cacophony of colors.

I scanned over the city, seeing buildings colored yellow ochre and burnt sienna or grey with stucco and mud, from the warm brown of the older wooden youth hostels to the newer European section with homes in muted puce, grey or salmon colors shimmering against the brilliant sky. Three-story skinny English houses in one section of the town stood apart in the distance. While in the center of Kathmandu a creamy white spire juxtaposed against the deep brown wood of intricately cut Tibetan temples and the dusty grey stone temple and statue of the Hindu monkey god Hanuman.. *Wow! I can't believe those are real monkeys roaming the grounds!*

The rounded top of a Tibetan Stupa, a mound of a holy Buddhist temple with a painted Buddha face on top and steps leading up to it with brightly colored flags on strings going out from the circumference, caught my eye first. *Is Buddha winking at me?* His eyes seemed to watch and follow me around.

The city was full of dichotomies. I saw the low top of an ornate lattice-work wooden Buddhist temple on the one hand and on the other hand a rounded white Muslim mosque towering over it like a phallic symbol. The better tourist hotels were right next to old youth hostels.

A primitive open market had stands of fruits, vegetables, materials, animals, and things I had never seen or heard of before. People seemed to be haggling about prices.

In the midst of the buzz, people were in motion. The streets themselves bustled with every mode of transportation from pedestrians, bicycles, cars, to rickshaws powered by a furiously peddling bicycle rider. These Nepalese bicyclers shimmered with sweat as they raced to make it to the next corner.

Some of the rickshaws could win races if only they were racing in the same direction. But there were cars, even European cars, like the Citron, small but economical, and then a few larger limousines or American-made sedans cruised the streets with what I imagined were VIPs.

It was a delight to the eye, Layla, and so much to take in at once, it almost looked unreal. Sensory overload!

The smells were of fresh dirt, vegetation, animals, fire, and spices as well as human sweat. Animals roamed the area, from large water buffalos to small dogs and something that looked like a donkey or pony. The people themselves varied from dark haired and dark skinned to a hodgepodge of white, red, black and yellow. The Nepalese were short compared to the stately, taller, Tibetans. Contrasts abounded from short Asians to the taller

German and Swiss tourists. There were only a few Americans at that time, but many of the people spoke English, thanks to the British.

I really stood out with my red hair and blue-green eyes. I was relieved to find this an advantage. People were curious about me, and communication was not hard, even if I had to gesture. The Nepalese language is very musical and sort of child-like, a lilting up-and-down kind of language with simple phrases that I managed to understand. The people were patient with me and with my awkward use of their language.

Tentatively I asked "*panee deenos*?" for "water please," and they responded by bringing me bottled water. *Success!* Then I said "*huncha*" for "thank you" or "good" (spelled like it sounds) and they smiled indulgently. When meeting someone new, I said "*Namaste*" which has an Indian meaning of "the spirit in me recognizes the spirit in you" and got a nod in response. *Isn't it amazing how you can make yourself understood with a bit of gestures, signs, motions or pictures, no matter what the language?*

I drew and snapped photos as much as possible. What I thought would be my main weakness in Nepal, not knowing the language, turned out not to be the case. It helped that I could draw and photograph, but I think there is an unspoken communication and intuitive sense from mind to mind that comes across if you are open to it. The important things I learned were things I could perceive, see, hear, taste, and feel about Kathmandu. And this contained a much more powerful truth than any guidebook ever written.

As I rode around Kathmandu in a rickshaw, I remembered how it all started and why I made the decision to come.

Nepalese in the market

4

Chapter Two

Teenage Heartbreak

B<small>Y THE TIME YOU READ THIS, MY DEAREST</small> L<small>AYLA, YOU WILL BE OLD</small> *enough to understand it and realize your grandma was all too human and pretty naïve as a teenager. Puberty meant confusing emotions, all related to the opposite sex. My mistake led to heartbreak. The reason I am so adamant about communicating now, no matter what the disaster, is because I had no one to talk about things to find out ahead of time what to do. In your own life you may make mistakes, but you have your family backing you up and there's always someone willing to share a little wisdom if you listen.*

Somewhere playing in my head was the song by the band The Who "It's Only Teenage Heartbreak" and I immediately thought of rolling down the hill with Gary.

As a teenager, I was so conflicted about things. My parents encouraged me to watch how I dressed and acted, but I was talking to my girlfriends about boys like they were a new species we had just discovered. Feeling inexperienced, awkward, but full of hormones we were mostly looking for fun, although what we sometimes found was trouble. Embarrassed to talk to some of the cute older boys, I searched for some way to start a conversation without looking spastic. *Did boys notice how I dressed? Was it dumb to want to put some makeup on? When a boy talked to me, should I just listen and smile? Or was that really lame? What kinds of things should I talk about? Do I act different if a boy is around? How am I suppose to act???*

It was not surprising that my first love was a boy who loved the outdoors, since that was what I liked talking about. Gary had red hair and blue eyes, a good looking combination on him. Too bad I was too naïve to see where it was going. Losing my virginity at sixteen didn't seem like a problem, since we were "in love." But at seventeen, not knowing enough about contraception and having to hide my relationship from my parents challenged me. The fun we had seemed worth the stress of sneaking around. We were so young we didn't think of consequences, but relished how alive we felt together. It was something new and exciting.

You are so fortunate to have a mom that you can talk to about anything, Layla, even about boys and sex. It wasn't a subject you talked about with parents in the seventies

We used to steal out to see each other as the sun went down, taking a sleeping bag with us into a wooded public park in the suburbs. That became our playground until that fateful night.

"What is it?" I asked Gary in a fearful voice, from inside the double sleeping bag. It was dark in the park, and we didn't realize we were on the top of a hill with trees going down to a lake. Then I heard something.

Gary said, "I see a flashlight coming this way. Duck down in the sleeping bag and be very quiet!" I was terrified, and thought we may have a stalker after us, so I rolled over a few times and so did Gary, and the next thing we knew we were tumbling down the hill still in our sleeping bag. It made a lot of noise, and I could hear someone coming. Uh, oh! Two police officers came up to us.

"Hey, you kids can't be here!" one of them said. "Do your parents know you're here?" the other one asked. *As if he really thought we would answer that one!* Gary tried to be polite, even though I knew he was scared. You see we were both naked inside the sleeping bag and only our heads and shoulders showed.

"Okay, officers, we'll go. We just need to change first," he said meekly. The officers caught on that we were naked and both started laughing.

"Good, but make it quick and don't let me catch you here again, or we'll let your parents know," the taller one said between chuckles. Never in my life have I put clothes on faster than I did that night. After thanking the officers with sheepish grins on our faces, we took off for the car and never looked back.

We didn't use a public park again for a long time. I think of that time whenever I see a double sleeping bag and laugh to myself imagining naked arms and legs sticking out tumbling down a hill, two people frantically trying hard to burrow down and disappear. Being too embarrassed to admit it, I still reach up to see if there are twigs and leaves in my hair when I think of it.

We had a wonderful summer until it all came crashing down so ruthlessly when I heard the news.

I feel numb. I can't think, can hardly breathe, and rocked by the news the nurse gave me a minute ago. I'm pregnant? *But I just was just seventeen a minute ago and in high school. This can't be right.*

"You used protection?" the nurse asked.

I shook my head.

"How long have you been sexually active?"

"With my boyfriend only, but for a year."

"And never any condoms or the pill?" her voice shrill with disbelief.

I felt suddenly wan, washed out. I shook my head again, tears stinging my eyes. I hated taking any pills. She was looking down at the paperwork.

Then in a softer voice, "But why, honey, why didn't you go to Planned Parenthood? They give free contraception to teens."

"I don't know. We used the rhythm method, abstaining at certain times. Never thought about it much and no one in my house speaks about sex…

Just thinking of them knots my stomach muscles and sets off a tremor in my knees. *What will my parents think? Say? Do?*

My parents had already kicked me out of the house as soon as I graduated high school because I was with Gary. We "shacked up" in a small apartment near my art college. *Will this be yet another blow for them?* I know they just couldn't deal with me having a boyfriend, and my mom seemed to prevent conversations about sex and never wanted to talk about it. *Maybe she couldn't handle it. Did she think it was a bad thing?* I remember crying in the bathroom when I was only thirteen, with my sister banging on the door to use the toilet, because I was bleeding so much "down there" and didn't know what was happening to me. I had to learn everything from my girlfriends--and from Gary.

❃ ❃ ❃

I know Gary needs to know about this latest development. *No pun intended.* So, I call him to meet me at our apartment "right now!"

Gary was in shock, his face a mask of seriousness. He said, with his voice cracking, that he had to discuss it with his mom. *His mother? Why didn't he just tell me he loves me, act happy, and ask me to marry him?* I told him, "Okay, but hurry back and tell your mom not to call my parents..

He does. When he comes back, he tells me with greater confidence. "My mom said to have an abortion, to just get rid of it. She says I'm too young to be a dad, and you have your whole art scholarship to think of. She says it's only the first trimester, and she knows a very good doctor..."

"Forget it, Gary! Just forget it. You and your mother are wrong. I will not kill my baby. Just go away. Forget it, forget us!" I shouted. His face crumples into a new mask, this time a sad, baffled one. Then I remembered, and say in a scared voice, "I have to go tell my parents before your mother does."

"I'll come with you."

He drives us, but I'm feeling completely alone and betrayed by him. He stays silent and I cry softly all the way. When I get to my parents' house I dry my eyes and try to act "normal."

I gather my parents in the living room and blurt out the news. The devastation on their faces is plain to see.

Then my mom says, "Oh, no! What will all my friends think?"

Really. She can worry about her bridge buddies at a time like this? There goes the second illusion, the one I've been carefully nurturing since finding out, the one about my parents wanting the baby and being somewhat excited. No way. Somehow I had the vague idea, a wish maybe, that they would jump at the chance to raise their grandchild. I know they love me, but the question is how much? But I know this is definitely testing their patience to the max with my rebellious, independent nature. I made a mistake, now I have to deal with it. But alone?

While talking this out with my parents, I feel like I'm not here. I'm out of my body and looking at some people deciding what I should do with my life. Suddenly I feel disconnected from Gary, from my parents, from life. I'm floating in a fog of hopelessness, as if my future is not my own.

My mom is a bit of a wreck, so my father steps in. "I'll help you handle this, Lynda. You can go to this home for unwedded mothers up north in Duluth and stay a couple months until your baby's born and then give it up for adoption. Everything will all be very quiet and comfortable. I'll pay for it, if Gary can't. I should have done something to break up the two of you a long time ago when I first suspected something was going on."

"It," he calls it an "it?" This is a child in here, not an "it." I'm feeling protective of my baby already and realize I do want to go away from here, from the criticism, from Gary's betrayal, from all of it. I need to sort it out on my own.

Gary came up to visit only once. It was dramatic and ended badly, with him wanting to have sex, but I refused. *My belly was too large, we were in a car, and he had abandoned me, so really what was he thinking!?* It was like almost drowning and trying to fight up to the surface again, the feeling of anger, hurt, and betrayal was so strong. I held it together until I returned to the home.

My savior was my roommate, Allison, who played guitar while still very pregnant herself. We sang and she played a great Bob Dylan song for me—"Any day now, any way now, I shall- be- re-leased."

When I gave birth after only three hours of labor, it was so effortless it seemed unreal. I was in this sterile hospital, all alone on a bed when they took the baby after I had my one chance to hug her.

I felt desperately sad for a time but told myself I had given something very precious of myself to the world and trusted that she would do well—better than with me. *Or with Gary!* I was letting someone else have the chance of raising the beautiful baby I created, people that could never have one of their own. It was my most selfless moment, but at the time it was still all so unreal for me.

I was glad when my dad came to fetch me shortly after that. I hated that hospital and never wanted to go in one if I could avoid it.

I decided right then the next time I was pregnant it would be with a supportive man and at home with a midwife, all cozy. You were born that way, my dearest Layla, because of your smart mom and dad. How do women do it in this strange, cold setting at a hospital?

And it was much too harsh for any young girl to face alone.

Chapter Three

Fresh Perspective

I DID HAVE A LOT OF TIME TO REALLY THINK OVER MY PRIORITIES AND struggled with what I wanted, what I was looking for. *Should I go back to art college? Do my parents still care about me? What do my friends think? Should I just take off? Am I going to be all right on my own now?* After I came back from Duluth, I knew I wanted to go back to college and decided to stay.

I met Gary only once when I got back, and he was very sorry, even embarrassed, and said he wanted me back. I was surprised as he pleaded with me and seemed to miss and love me. But I had grown up that summer, did not love him anymore, and for once he was at a loss. *What did I really see in him before? Did I think he would stand behind me? Was I disappointed to learn he was weak, surprised that he was doing what his mom said instead, or that he couldn't be counted on? What did I expect?* I looked at him differently now and was determined this would not permanently hurt me. Not jaded by the experience, I decided to be more discerning and self-reflective now. *What good would it do to mope about it? It was a devastating time, but I really did what I thought best. I wanted to move on now and create something better.*

Enrolled in the Minneapolis College of Art, I immersed myself in the world of art, working hard that first year. I had an excellent drawing and painting teacher who had his own oil paintings in museums, so I avidly listened and studied under him. Also I took photography classes, sculpture, art history and humanities. It was refreshing not having to listen to the usual psychobabble my friends had to listen to in regular universities, and I was able to concentrate upon painting and drawing. I had already seen what it was like at a university with large groups staring at a screen or lecturer, mindlessly memorizing information they never used.

It is worse today, Layla, and you will find that only a few colleges really intern students to apply the knowledge they gain. The doing is the important thing—what you do with the principles, theories, or ideas in your life.

I was so happy at an art college where you *did* what you learned. The only humanities class I took was with a bright professor who gave a current topic and had us stand up and give our views. Then the group would discuss it. He gave us reading assignments geared to make you think, and he was tolerant of other opinions while pointing out any flaws in an argument. *What about the Vietnam war? Who started it, and what was it really about? Who benefits from the war? How do you feel about draft dodgers?* He made it lively and fun. Learning came alive for me.

Finding out how things work in the Arts involves some physics, anatomy, composition, use of light and shadow, complementary colors, the use of the vanishing points and horizon line in a landscape, measurements, how to make things look three dimensional, and much more. There was science to art. It was a very busy and joyful time. I was finally doing what I loved most!

During that time, I knew I needed to find some answers so I checked out spiritual paths. *What did people think of God or a higher power? How does that help them?* I attended services at Baptist, Lutheran, Catholic, and Protestant churches as well as a Jewish Bar Mitzvah. I made the scene at New Age gatherings; some included meditation, yoga, hypnotism (which didn't work on me), and some had a few psychedelic drugs thrown in. The drugs were deemed "mind altering" and there was one moment it opened up a whole new world to me. Trouble was after a drug trip you always had to come down to the hum-drum world and face reality. I wanted to find an exciting life of discovery and inquiry, but it was quite a while before I came to the conclusion that drugs were *not* "the answer" to anything, no matter how good they made you feel while you were taking them.

In the seventies many young people experimented with drugs, and it had a very powerful pull, Layla. But think about it, what happens when you come down? Would you then have to take a drug forever to stay high? I was dumb enough to try it, but in my lucid moments realized I didn't really need them.

This was not the last time that drugs dulled my interest in life and hope for finding my own path.

Drugs were a detour that I should have avoided. I was not smart enough then to realize that I was dabbling in unreality trying to find out what was real.

My enthusiasm returned when, after my first year in college, I gained a scholarship to England as an exchange student in the arts. All I had known of the world was found in Minnesota and Wisconsin with a few vacation trips with family to Washington DC and the Ozarks. But even America in its entirety is only a small part of the planet I was standing on, and I wanted to get out and explore it all and see for myself. I was ready. Before, I was not sure what I wanted.

No hesitation anymore, by God!

Chapter Four

Eleventh Hour Rescue

J UST THE THOUGHT OF GOING TO SCHOOL IN LONDON ON AN ART SCHOL-
*arship was exhilarating enough, Layla, but going across on an ocean liner
to Europe made it much more perfect.*

I packed a trunk full of clothes for the voyage. I was going with a group of
American students on the S.S. Stattendam for six days across the Atlantic. It
turned out to be a joyous trip on that big ship leaving from New York harbor.

Traveling to New York on my own was a thrill, going into Manhattan after
landing, with the many famous skyscrapers and bridges I recognized all
crowded onto this small island of land. I loved the action of people walking
by in droves. Every age group talking, crossing the intersections quickly
with taxis honking, and street vendors haggling, some with a deep accent.
The amount of different nationalities, people of all countries in one place,
captured my attention. The shops with brightly lit and artfully done window
displays enticed me to get something, even though I had no need. That was
the point, of course. Finally we met up and were herded onto the ocean liner
in the huge harbor, with the Statue of Liberty in the distance. Too soon we
left New York behind and headed for open water.

There were thirty of us, about half boys and half girls, chosen as exchange
students from all over the States, going to England and various universities
abroad. It was an enchanting time, traveling on an ocean liner and being
courted by several good-looking male students, teasing, laughing, and
drinking Drambuie for the first time. (In Scottish, this word means "the
drink that satisfies.") We avoided being sea sick and watched the ocean at

night from the stern. *It felt so liberating. What would Europe hold for us? How could anything harm us when we felt so young and carefree? We were indestructible!*

Laughing, we played music, cards and charades, danced, and talked about hopes and dreams, staying up late into the night—a raucous group all the way across the Atlantic. Finally, on the sixth day we saw the Irish cliffs by Cobb with that unbelievable green that only an island drenched in rain and surrounded by water can achieve.

Docking finally in Southampton, England, I stared over at all the hustle and bustle of dock workers in one of the busiest ports in the world, and felt goose bumps rise up on my arms with shivery thrills running up and down my spine as I took in the landscape, one that seemed foreign yet familiar.

Chapter Five

Viewing Life through Art

Y*OU HAVE TO REMEMBER, LAYLA, THAT THE EUROPEANS HAVE BEEN around for many more centuries before America was founded and they feel proprietary in some ways, even though most of the time they were fighting wars! To me England felt like an older brother taking a young sister under his wing.*

The English students called me a "colonialist" when they first met me at Wimbledon College of Art near London. But they did it in an endearing paternal way the English have for their "subjects", so I was not really offended. I landed on the student council as the foreign representative. *It may have had something to do with the fact I was going out with the good-looking president of the student council.* Mathew didn't patronize me, had a kind manner, and was a wonderful escort, orienting me in a new country.

"Your hair is a great shade of red," he told me as I looked at his startlingly thick good-looking premature grey, almost white, hair and just laughed.

"Yours is cool, too. I like an older man!" I told him (*he was twenty-one*).

Settling in with an English family, the school in the States had arranged room and board. I found them friendly, but a little aloof. I was so busy with college I was rarely there anyway so it worked out well for all of us.

Learning printmaking using the huge stones in the traditional way it was done for a hundred years and crafting sculpture or pottery with red clay was so much fun. There are many craftsmen's and artisan's techniques that should be taught before they become lost in time. *With no one to pass along the techniques and no one learning them in art schools, they will eventually become a lost art,* I thought to myself with dismay. It made me double my effort to learn the techniques.

I decided I had to see London the first month I was there. The area I entered getting off the subway was so delightfully English. The skinny three-story houses, ornate street lamps and the large stone buildings from hundreds of years ago, gave the impression that London was ageless. Buildings with a lot of stone and brickwork, moldings and cornices with decorative touches you just don't see any more. I was looking at history; hundreds of years before my country. I soaked it all in.

"Excuse me, where is the Royal Academy of Art?" I asked an older Scottish gentleman.

"Right over there, miss," he responded. "American, right?"

"Yes, I'm over here on exchange to Wimbledon Art College. But I'd really like to see any new developments in the art world while I'm in London. I already saw all the museums," I said with frustration. He got my meaning.

"Well, why don' ya go o'rr to the Ex'perimenta' College. Just a'cross the street. There!" he said pointing. "Might find it a wee bit more excit'n," he said with more of the Scottish burr coming out.

Off I went across the street from the Royal Academy of Art and entered the Experimental College. What I saw made my eyes widen. I could feel my ears ring and a slight throbbing in my head. I was hit with so many sounds and new ideas at once it took a moment to catch my breath in front of the entrance.

There before me was a series of machines that several students and a teacher were fiddling with. They ranged in size from a large cabinet to a small instrument. The noises I heard varied from animal sounds, human singing, orchestras to street noises and other sounds I couldn't figure out. Some melodious, some discordant like a traffic jam.

After introductions, I starting asking a lot of questions, and a man I thought may be the teacher came over to help. He showed me one machine which had knobs and dials on it, with an oscilloscope showing a wave pattern in a window on the front. It was an "envelope shaper" and the wave patterns were frequency waves. You could change the wave pattern with a dial and thereby change the sound. He showed me how a voice or a normal sound from the street could be shaped—elongating the rise and fall of the wave to stretch it out, so to speak, or squeeze it in closer, and change the sounds dramatically. You could record anything, natural sounds or not, and then feed it into the machine which then could manipulate the sound in any of a number of ways.

"Here, go ahead and try it. Speak into the recorder." The man who I thought was a teacher held up a microphone.

I tried it on my voice and sure enough, once recorded in the machine, I could then make it sound totally different like bird songs, animal howls, or a supernova.

Amazing!

"This is so cool! You can do anything you want with sounds!" I said to him, feeling my face flush.

"You're an artist, so maybe you can appreciate this. I may show you where it all started," he said in a mysterious voice I took as a challenge.

"I want to see everything. Please! I want to understand it all," I told him.

He seemed proud and happy to show me where he worked, where his machine was originally built, and called his inventions "electronic music machines."

He told me some engineers had been working on this for years now. But he had the advantage of being in London and was a musician as well as an engineer. He also tuned large pipe organs, which is a very precise art.

I followed him across the way to a large church. Going down to the basement level, I first saw his machines as well as the bottom part of a pipe organ with tubes sticking up through the ceiling to the main floor above. Apparently pipe organs have the most awesome ranges of sound and can be tuned to emit different frequencies, which translate into different musical sounds. I was caught up in all this and we talked for a long time. At the end before I had to leave, he told me about an exhibit coming up that I shouldn't miss.

John Cage was giving a demonstration of different electronic music on three or four stages in a huge hall in London. Of course, I went to see it and, yes, as I wandered from stage to stage it struck me that I was observing the start of a new technology--a new development in music. Not long after that, musicians of all kinds were checking out the applications of this art.

What I stumbled upon was the start of synthesizers in performance art and electronic music.

Thirst for knowledge was always a driving force and led to many decisions I made, intuitively or impulsively, to find out something for myself. I was fortunate to be in the right place at the right time and to be so curious.

There is only so much you can read about before you get the itch to go out and find it!

Chapter Six

Chasing Simon

A S YOU GROW UP, MY BEAUTIFUL LAYLA, BOYS WILL FLOCK AROUND YOU *at eighteen. I found one of the most complicated loves of my life in a foreign land. For you my fervent wish is you will find and know the right man when you meet him, wherever that may be—and not be so easily distracted by men like your grandmamma!*

I met him on the ceiling, soon after I arrived in England.

Crazy with curiosity to get to know London more, I often rode into the city on the subway. Posters for the London Exhibition of Modern Furniture Designs caught my eye and I headed right for it. Inside the exhibition, on one of the display beds, I saw a man lying there staring up into the intricately mirrored ceiling above him. As I looked up into the ceiling mirror, our eyes met.

It seemed like things went still for a moment. There he was looking up, but to me it appeared he was looking down at me sprawled out on the bed below. We both smiled into the mirror-faces of each other. We looked intently at each other that way, looming above our bodies, for a few lingering seconds. Then found each other in the flesh as he sat up, stood and smiled at me.

Did he like me? Who was this mysterious guy and how did he happen to be here? Were we meant to meet?

Simon was of average build, good-looking with long glossy black hair, in a pony tail, with deep-set dark eyes and a trim beard. Later, I was to find out that he was very particular about his hair and how he groomed it. It was his intense, intelligent eyes that first captivated me. With his olive skin you could tell his family was Spanish by descent and although he was not tall, he gave off the air of strength. I liked that about him—that power in reserve.

He told me later that it was my green eyes and red hair that first captured him. Next, he told me, he was attracted by my tight American jeans and full-length, fitted brown velvet, double-breasted coat—the latest fashion in London at the time and my first purchase in England.

Wow, I've only been in London a few hours and already I'm falling in love?!

He opened his mouth and in an English accent said, "A wonderful exhibit, don't you think? My name's Simon, by the way. You came to the right place to have a bit of fun. Here, let me show you around. I think you'll like it over on this side," he said with a gleam in his eye and a curl of a smile on his lips.

Is he for real? Does he really mean me?

Despite being distracted by our shoulders touching from time to time as he showed me around, I was amazed at the details of the futuristic "rooms" they had erected in the middle of London. We spent time going through the rooms together, joking and generally getting to know each other. I was always the excited, buoyant one in a group and Simon seemed a little surprised at some of my enthusiastic reactions to the exhibit and interest in him.

"I usually deal with dry philosophy professors and bored students," he explained.

"And not bubbly, adventurous American women, huh?" I replied.

He smiled. It wasn't long before I found out he went to college at Oxford and majored in philosophy. He was a bit older than I, and was just starting his graduate training under a professor.

I told him that I was studying at the School of Art in Wimbledon and had already seen part of London by the Royal Academy of Art across the street from the Experimental College. I talked to him about meeting the guy who built electronic music machines and how lucky I was that he took me over to the basement of his church. I told Simon about playing with the electronic equipment while the electronic music teacher talked, both of us testing out in practice what he was saying in theory.

Simon seemed genuinely interested, and said he loved music and had a huge record collection covering the whole wall of his apartment. "This is where John Cage got his start," Simon told me.

I mentioned the Cage experimental music event in London I had just seen. But at the moment I wanted to see more of the world and more of Simon.

He opened up and started telling me about his travels through Europe to Morocco. "The only thing that I didn't like about traveling to Morocco was getting malaria. Malaria is something you can never fully get rid of, but I have it under control. I never regret going to Morocco, though." He described the city, the Arab people dressed in robes and head pieces, open markets with exotic sights, smells and sounds, selling everything you could imagine in an Arab country. We talked a long time.

Intensely interested in each other, we continued our conversation over dinner at an English pub and later in his apartment. Intrigued by exotic places, I listened to every word. Eventually after coming over to see him for a few days I told him about myself and my own travels in the States. He was interested in everything American. He listened like he was trying to absorb my psyche, but I also felt there was a definite physical spark between us, increasing all the time. Later our absorption was mutually physical as well and we finally made love with a rare passion.

He was a considerate lover, starting slow, kissing and touching me until everything tingled. Eventually our clothes were gone, and he was on top of me looking at me with those intense eyes while we slowly made love, moving effortlessly with the flow.

I wonder even now what he was really thinking. I felt the overwhelming sensations we created together, the friction as well as the light touches. It was too much to resist at the time, but then I didn't really try to resist it.

I thought I was "in love." My hormones were working overtime, overwhelming any logical thought. At the time I remember I loved how it made me stop thinking and I was suddenly only feeling.

Chapter Seven

London Lament

M Y DAYS AND NIGHTS WERE FILLED FROM THEN ON WITH LOVING Simon. I was still enrolled at the London Art College, but stayed at Simon's flat in London for several months and traveled back and forth from the college. We ended up either in his bedroom making love or being domestic—cooking, as well as playing some of his vast music collection while indulging in smoking a little grass or going out to sample the London cuisine.

Simon loved his English tea, especially with sugar and milk in certain exact proportions. He also liked doing Tarot Card readings for fun, a hobby of his. When I drew the "hanged man" card, which looked very ominous to me, he shrugged and told me, "This represents both danger and opportunity. It's up to you which it will be."

The Tarot cards have a lot of significance and so much is left up to interpretation. The impression I got was that the cards were based upon mythology, seeming to come from the world of magic and maybe psychic gypsies! But playing cards were used by George Washington and also I read they were used during World War II to pass along coded information disguised in a game. I liked that part, and for us it was all in good fun, although Simon seemed to take it seriously.

They are really just cards, my Layla, so don't believe everything you hear. You make your own future.

I never dwelled upon it too much at the time, but at least I had a choice and decided that I was in for an opportunity!

Another thing Simon liked to do was test me on classical music. I had some experience with classical guitar, since Gary, my high school boyfriend, played and we once saw Andre Segovia play. But Simon liked to put a classical piece on his tape machine, from his vast collection of music, and asked me who it was after playing a few bars.

"Sibelius? Vivaldi? Beethoven? Which is it?" he asked. If I guessed right, he smiled and made me feel I had passed some kind of test. He was an assistant professor after all, so he was in that mind set. Unfortunately, if I got it wrong, I felt like a dunce. He wanted to share this with me, but at the same time I felt treated like a child instead of being asked all about what I like or think. To him maybe I was a child. It's funny I never thought of testing him on the Arts, the laws of perspective, composition, or the color wheel. *I wonder how well he would have done if the tables were reversed? I think you may find, Layla, men that ask about what you think or know are more interesting than those that show off.*

I started to feel a bit intimidated by him and his slightly condescending attitude. It annoyed me and I began to think about leaving for a while. Also, I had a premonition that our relationship wouldn't last. The concrete reason I gave him for wanting to leave and go back to the States concerned a phone call from a man I knew from Seattle. It was a very unexpected, but fateful call.

Chuck, a sweet young man who just came back from the war and was staying with mutual friends in Minnesota, was someone I had had a relationship with before I left for England. He had cried out to me by phone that he was in big trouble. Strung out from being in Vietnam where he saw his best friend cut in half by a misplaced missile, he was desperate for comfort and love. He called me numerous times when I was in England, saying he couldn't live without me. Gullible that I was, after he begged for the third time that he "needed me" that he was "dying without me" and I should come back to him immediately, I felt I could not abandon him. I really thought he might even commit suicide and didn't want to be the reason for that, so I agreed to go back to the States.

Leaving Simon's house, before I changed my mind, I opened the door to a rainstorm so intense it felt like the city was crying. Simon stood there stoic but I could tell he was sad and really didn't want me to go. We kissed and held each other with renewed purpose just inside the doorway. Besides the rain, the soulful, sad instrumental song, *Samba Pa Ti*, by Santana was playing in the background. It had been our song. Our time had been one of innocence and passion, but I felt a strong pull from home and had to leave.

Would I ever see him again?

Chapter Eight

Ticket to Ride

WHEN I WENT TO JOIN CHUCK IN SEATTLE, MY INTENTION WAS TO HELP *him, but instead I was drawn into his world. The lure of drugs is so strong for many people, Layla, so you should know what could happen and actually did to me.*

Chuck was deeply influenced by his buddies from Vietnam and some were strung out on hard drugs. We became romantically involved and way too much for my own good. His dark world was slowly dragging me down. Not knowing much about it made me too vulnerable. I wish I could have predicted better where it was going, but at the time I was caught up in it. My parents didn't want to get involved and I thought they couldn't help me, even if they did know. *What did I get myself into now?*

After a few weeks Chuck got caught holding a lid of marijuana (nicknamed "grass") and was unwise enough to be standing next to a big time dealer at the time of a raid. He was arrested and put in jail. They didn't charge me but took me into the station too and put me in a cell. The police scared me numb with possible jail time because I was with him at the time. They called my parents and said I could leave the next day. The judge had a talk with me, warning me never to get into this kind of situation again with drug dealers. *I didn't realize how prophetic his advice was. How could I get out of this trap I seemed to be in and still help Chuck?*

We both ended up flying back to Minnesota. He came after me when his jail time was up. He tried out a few jobs but after a couple months Chuck was again immersed in the drug culture in North Minneapolis thanks to his "friends."

What kind of "friends" push dope on you, anyway?

At first he really did try to find a job, but no one seemed to be hiring hippies, especially to work in an office. He was more interested in an outdoor job anyway, but those were scarce in the city. North Minneapolis was cheap to live in, but not the safest place, as I found out. It was full of druggies.

I got a job to support us in a bar and restaurant, The Five, owned by a five- member band that did cover songs. They were actually pretty good and played popular rock songs on the weekends. After having to wear black hot pants, a white sleeveless shirt and black heels, I was relieved to take off my "uniform" after work and count my tips. It was good pay, but after a while getting beer spilled on me, having to dance around the tables with a full tray of food to avoid knocking into someone on the crowded dance floor, and hearing the same songs over, and over again, that was it. *No more "Jeremiah was a bullfrog" for me!* The tips were the only thing holding me there. I had to finish Art College to get into the kind of job I wanted. This was temporary and paid the bills, but after a few months it all became too much.

Chuck's buddies were strung out. I was trying to paint at this time, but my real value was helping—getting two people off drugs—a girlfriend of mine and Chuck's friend, David.

David was married to a pretty blonde who taught kindergarten. I was upset about how his addiction was tearing his family apart. His young wife was at her wits end trying to figure out how to help him off drugs as he kept sneaking out to his buddies' apartment. One day Chuck and I were at a party and I was the only one in the room of a dozen people who was sober. I saw David shooting up heroin. He was nodded off, rocking back into a dead sleep. Everyone else looked mildly asleep or in a drug haze. But David went chalk white with a drugged look much deeper and stronger than warranted, and I thought, "He may never come back this time!"

Jumping up, I grabbed David and dragged him around the room until he starting walking on his own. I poured coffee down his throat, reviving him a bit. This walk/coffee routine went on for some time until finally he seemed to wake up out of his stupor. Another person staggered awake and started to help me. By then, he could eat and sit up and was well enough to be on his own. He recovered, to my great relief. Had I not been there, he would have over-dosed and died right there in that room, surrounded by all his friends totally out of it on drugs and oblivious to any danger.

Shortly after that close call, a girlfriend, Shelly, tripped out on some strong LSD, and I got a call from the University of Minnesota Emergency Hospital. *Drug overdoses are more common now, Layla, and not knowing how much a body can take is often fatal.* Apparently, she had my number to contact since she had no family here, and the doctor was holding her to see if she came down from the drugs or not on her own. When I got to the hospital they told me they were going to have to commit her to a mental ward if she didn't snap out of it. The very words, "mental ward" sounded ominous to me. After all, I'd seen *One Flew Over the Cuckoo's Nest,* so I was afraid for her since earlier I had heard stories about people being put into psychiatric wards: given drugs and electro-shock and never coming out alive!

I ended up talking the doctor into letting me help her first, since she had no immediate family. Carefully going into her room, I found her wandering around, staring at everything with that far-away drugged look. She did not even acknowledge there were other people around, just talked out loud to something unseen, wandered back and forth, staring off and never making eye contact, occasionally crying out or shouting something unintelligible.

I instinctively mimicked all her motions, went with her around the room silently doing everything she did—even going into the shower with all my clothes on when she did. After over two hours of this, she abruptly looked at me. I had hope. Then she grunted at me, at least noticing I was there, and little by little she began to focus in on me.

Finally I spoke and said "Hi." She looked at me strangely, but nodded. As I quietly followed her around further, she became more comfortable with me, less drugged looking and more alert.

In a short while she said, "Where did you come from?" like I had just appeared out of thin air, *which in her mind, maybe I did*! Then I was able to get more and more into communication with her. An hour later she was ready to leave the hospital. The doctor, who was extremely overworked and stressed with a line-up of patients in the standing-room-only waiting room, but took the time to talk to me. He admitted that those waiting patients were in worse shape than my friend, dismissing her to my care. I was greatly relieved and able to take her home. Later, she told me I had saved her life, but I wasn't so sure. The experience, however, made me decide to avoid psychedelic drugs as well as hospitals.

Then I finally had my own bad drug experience. You couldn't call it horrible, since I wasn't seeing monsters or anything. Chuck had talked me into trying something new that he'd scored.

You would think that seeing David almost die and seeing my friend out of her mind would have been warning enough, but that's the sad thing, Layla, it wasn't. The magnet pull of drugs is real, seductive, and the desire for sensation insatiable, mainly because we were so young and wanted to experience everything. But the stupidity was that you really didn't need them to feel or enjoy life. I didn't find that out for quite a while, however.

He convinced me by telling me, "This is powerful stuff, but it's okay. I'm taking it myself. I really want you to join me and experience what I do. I love you and really want us to be closer." I was so gullible at that point I said I would try "a little." He got out a syringe, put some powder in a spoon, added a little water, and lit a match under the spoon to heat the solution and make it dissolve. Then he sucked the new liquid into a syringe. He tied-off my arm with a long thin rubber strap and slowly pricked the vein of my arm inside the bend of my elbow and slid in the needle. I wasn't really looking, but it didn't hurt much. I thought maybe it would be nothing.

The next thing I knew I was on the floor, leaning against the wall, feeling like I had floated away in a timeless dream. I felt all fuzzy in the head when I awoke to find four people staring down at me in horror. Chuck looked like the color of my titanium white oil paints and his terrified eyes had black pupils with no blue showing now. I wondered what all the fuss was about. *Where did I go?*

"Lynda, are you alright? I thought we lost you for good, you were gone so long!" he said with trembling voice. "I didn't realize how pure the stuff was and gave you too much. I was so scared, you could have died and it would have been all my fault!" He seemed to be pleading with me to forgive him.

I only nodded at him and said, "I just need to lie down for a little while... By myself," I added, a little shaky and confused.

During that time, I did try some other milder things, but even the grass or amphetamines, were pulling me down. I didn't feel myself and had to struggle to get a grip on things. There were some nice highs, and I felt energetic—until I came down from the drugs. It even affected my painting, the thing I loved doing more than anything in my life. After taking a drug I felt lethargic and didn't want to paint anymore. I had trouble *doing* things. The drugs started to take away my ambition, and put me into a placid, lackadaisical mood. This was not "me." Somehow I knew I needed to get away from this or I would smother. My whole spirit, as well as my life, was at risk.

Occasionally during that time I'd write letters to Simon in England and the. to him in Canada, where he was now teaching. Simon had moved and was an assistant professor of philosophy in Halifax, Nova Scotia, before his permanent position at the University in Toronto, Canada. The last communication to him was on a tape I sent him of just me talking. It was right after the almost-overdose, and I was feeling extremely low. Apparently my voice matched my apathetic mood. It was weak and he told me later, didn't sound like me at all. The tape freaked him out. He thought I was going to die where I was, surrounded by druggies. I got a letter back within days with an airplane ticket in it. He insisted I join him in Canada. His intention was strong; his command nonnegotiable.

Simon saved my life at the time, I'm sure of it. I used that ticket and left Chuck a day or two later, suggesting he leave and go back to his home town in Seattle. *Would he really get off drugs now? I hope he finds his way, but I can't stay here anymore. It's slowly killing me.*

I remembered the lyrics to that old Bob Dylan song, *"She's got everything she needs, she's an artist, she don't look back."*

Chapter Nine

Canada Cross Country

MY ESCAPE TO CANADA HAPPENED QUICKLY. I WAS SOON FLYING OVER to the east coast to the Atlantic Ocean, north of Maine's shoreline by about five-hundred miles, and there it was; Halifax, Nova Scotia.

I was on my way to see Simon again. A little anxious, I wondered how he would feel about my leaving him in England and hooking up with another man. *Did he still love me? Would he be jealous or supportive? Could we really build a relationship on more than sex?* I still loved him and hoped he felt the same, but I was not so sure yet and kept picking at my food on the plane, feeling nervous with very little appetite. I needn't have worried. He was there to pick me up when the plane landed and looked at me with friendly eyes while giving me a big hug.

"Hi, I'm glad you made it. So good to see you again!" he smiled while saying this. He seemed really happy to see me. *Maybe he didn't think he would ever see me alive again!*

Halifax is a quaint fishing village on the Atlantic Ocean and full of the hustle and bustle of small town life with many of the buildings right on the waterfront. When Simon drove me around to orient me, I could see Cape Breton to the north, the imposing promontory that rose up more than a thousand feet from the shoreline, and shining emerald green at the top with grass and plant life. It reminded me so much of Ireland or Scotland I immediately wanted to paint it. After arriving I went with Simon to a Scottish bagpipe festival up there. It was eerie but melodious at the same time with haunting bagpipe music echoing off the water. It created a magical feeling. I began to relax into the familiar comfort of being with Simon.

Sharing a small apartment with Simon in Halifax, I went to the local art college while Simon taught at the University there as an assistant professor in philosophy. We made friends and went out on the weekends. Also we found two Siamese kittens and adopted the male, naming him "Sammy". He was smart and frisky, amusing us endlessly with his antics. One of my girlfriends, an airline stewardess for Air Canada, took us to the fishing boats and we bought several large lobsters for a dollar each on my birthday. We boiled them in large pots at the beach bonfire with melted butter and had a grand seafood party. I fell in love with lobster and swore to have it for my birthday every year from that point on.

One time Simon invited a handful of his senior students from the college over to our house. He smoked a little grass and drank alcohol with them and asked them all kinds of questions, letting them discuss points of philosophy. At the time in the seventies, that seemed normal but probably not College policy. *It did get some interesting viewpoints, I'd have to say—probably more interesting than most political debates! But it was a shame it had to happen when they were high. What could they come up with if sober?*

Just before the summer, Simon said he had to fly back to England to see his family for a week. Also he was honest enough to let me know he was going to stay in a place with his old girlfriend, Freda. He had talked a lot about her, and even when he said she had a new boyfriend now, I felt there was still a pull there. The house they were staying at was huge and had plenty of room. I didn't say much when he left. I started to think he was never coming back. *I really believed he was getting back together with his old flame.*

To distract myself, I attended an acting workshop and joined a performance group in Nova Scotia. It was so fun and in a little theater with a small group of performers in the main company. I met someone there, a very handsome tall, brown-haired guy with light eyes and a happy disposition. He made me laugh so much! I realized the effects of the time with Chuck introverted me. This young man, Brian, was just what I needed—extroversion and romance! It only lasted a week or ten days, but when Simon was due back Brian asked me if I would stay with him. He and the acting company wanted me to perform with them and help out on the production sometimes and use my art. He said he loved me and wanted to live with me, traveling around the country on tour. It did sound exciting and tempting. He was romantic and fun to be with, and he made me feel important as he truly complimented my work and my art. I really cared about him. *But most importantly, he really valued me as I was and didn't want to change me.*

I had a big choice to make, and I didn't feel quite experienced enough to make the right one. Talking it over with Simon when he got back, I found out he had ended it with Freda, was just tying up some loose ends in England and was devastated that I had another boyfriend. He and I paced back and forth, walking all over the city that night, talking with heart-wrenching honesty about what we should do. He vowed that he wanted me, wanted to be with me from then on. I tried to lessen the hurt I knew he was feeling and told him I honestly thought he was getting back with Freda when he left me for England. He was so anguished and upset that I knew I could not leave him now. Making my decision, I told him that I'd break off with Brian and was ready to make our relationship work.

In a most intimate meeting with Brian, kissing him, crying with him and facing his sorrow with doubts of my own about the future, I told Brian, " I just can't leave Simon. Not now."

He accepted it with grace, but told me, "This is the worst thing that's happened to me. I will think of you always and wish you were with me." He said it so sincerely I couldn't breathe without aching for him. I had to just take it all in, hold it in my heart and mind as I silently sent my thoughts out to him. As I started walking away, I pleaded with him in my mind. *I know what you mean. I will remember you always, too, and think of you performing to the audience, delighting the girls with the way you smile, joking with friends and making everyone laugh like you do no matter what's happening. This is the hardest decision for me, but I think it's the right one. Please understand.* He was man enough to let me go, but I sometimes wonder what my life would be like if I had gone with him.

But then, I might never have married your grandpa which means that I may never have met you, Layla.

I went to Simon and told him of my decision. We embraced and renewed our bonds with each other, vowing to stay together no matter what. Simon was fierce in his declaration as I cried and held him that night.

Besides loving him, Simon saved my life, and I owed him for that.

Chapter Ten

Outdoor Therapy

For Simon it was summer break from his teaching so we packed up the International Harvester van with our things and took Sammy, our Siamese cat, and went on the road across Canada. The van was fitted with a double bed in the back and a small fridge with a portable Coleman cooking stove and supplies. We were set for several months and drove many long hours across the changing scenery of Canada which reminded me of northern Minnesota. From Algonquin Park, with its tall pine trees and foliage in full bloom, to the flat plains of Saskatchewan, we traveled west to the Rockies. Banff was our goal, and we stopped for supplies so our backpacks were ready. *Being outdoors is great therapy for me!*

Such a spectacular area, climbing the mountains to get to the upper meadows gave us the view from left to right of a series of high mountains, some snowcapped, alive with such a burst of plant life down below it startled the eyes. *For as far as you can see, the beauty of summer mountains in full bloom all around us—yellow, blue, purple, and pink wild flowers like carpets so soft you wanted to sink into them, snuggle down and sleep in them protected by the giant peaks and all the while breathing in the splendor of the clear blue sky above.*

We had a canoe on a carrier on top of the van, and even Sammy cat was content to ride with us and in the canoe later on. He was a most unusual cat. When we parked we took it down and spent the next month canoeing, camping on the banks of a lake, or struggling with a portage to the next body of water in a string of lakes in Alberta near the Banff-Jasper highway.

That was the summer I really learned to appreciate native cultures, living off the land. The awareness that we were living in harmony with the nature around us finally set in. This is what it must have been like to be living off the land like native people even as our ancestors did. We would catch rainbow trout for breakfast and pick wild berries, and set up the tent near the lake shore. One day, I swear it was in broad daylight, we had a tent up near a sandbar on the lake. Hearing a wild sound, we looked over and a baby moose came out of the trees along with its large mother. They were running for their life across the sand bar to the other side of the lake. It was only thirty feet from us, and suddenly a large black bear came running after them crossing the sand bar. They all took off into the woods on the other side, leaving us frozen in place watching where they had just come from and thinking— *are we safe here?*

We saw many bears on the shore, some with cubs, and bald eagles swooped down sometimes, following us as we rowed almost soundlessly on the lake. Simon and I always hung up our food at night so the bears couldn't get it. One especially memorable night there was snorting and sounds of a bear outside our tent. Simon cautiously crept out to see what was going on and saw a large bear pawing around trying to reach our food. He used his flashlight and shouted a bit to scare him off.

The bears were not the tame kind that frequent the parks in the States and fortunately didn't like to be around people and took off. The squirrels, birds, ducks, and loons talked to us when we set up camp at night. The peace was not all quiet, but felt infinitely safe and somehow freeing.

We talked, sang, laughed, kissed, made love, ate and rowed our way through that wonderful month on the lakes. I became so trim and fit, after so much canoe rowing and hiking, and was so red-tan I looked like an Indian myself. But it was near the end of our journey.

Our Siamese, Sammy (short for Samuel P. Tat) hunted every night we made camp. He brought us a nice mouse he caught and showed it off, then ate it. He was so happy out in the wilds. One night, however, very deep in the woods we heard a loud growling noise far off and that night Sammy didn't come back. It was three long nights, with us calling his name, searching for him, until we had to go. I was so devastated. It was like losing my child all over again. *My baby! I realized that Sammy was like our child.* It reminded me too much of the child I lost. I cried so hard and for so long I think Simon got annoyed and he couldn't understand.

We both loved Sammy dearly and had raised him from a kitten. He was a very smart and good looking cat, a mix and not too skinny with seal point markings and a striped tail with big blue eyes. He looked up when we talked to him, made the right moves to get understood, and generally became part of the family. Cats have a way of snuggling up, purring, and making you feel better, calmer. *Therapeutic!* Sammy had that ability. I knew Simon was very hurt too, but finally we both couldn't take it anymore and decided we needed to go. *Good-bye, Sammy, wherever you are.*

I felt a foreboding, like losing Sammy had severed our relationship in an un-alterable way. *Like losing a child we could never get back.*

When we got to Victoria on Vancouver Island, Chuck came up from Seattle to meet us. He had never met Simon, and I was nervous about the reaction. Chuck had gotten off drugs and was working as a carpenter in Marysville, Washington, and just started dating his sweetheart from high school. I was happy for him and had invited him to join us on our vacation.

I knew Simon was curious about him, and when they met they couldn't have been more different. Chuck, with long blonde hair, blue eyes, tall and slender, was a country boy. Simon on the other hand was the dark and intense intellectual. But they seemed to get along, and we pitched two tents, changed into swim suits, me in my new low-cut, one-piece white swimsuit, and dove into the clear waters of the stream near the campsite. After the swim we stayed up making a fire, talking, eating and drinking until the wee hours. I had a few second thoughts, and there was some banter back and forth in a bit of one-upmanship between the two men. As it got later, I went from one tent to the other tent, spending time with Chuck and then Simon. Chuck had changed and I saw the things I really loved about him, how sweet he was to me. Simon was putting up a good front, somewhat reserved and making the best of the situation, but I could tell he was not totally comfortable with it. By the time it was midnight, I finally dropped into my sleeping bag in Simon's tent, after a good night kiss on the cheek from Chuck. It was confusing for me, but I thought I was making the right choice staying with Simon.

The next day, we had to go and I was a little sad at the parting. Later that day, when we were again on the mainland and driving away from Vancouver, I remembered it. *Oh No! I forgot my swim suit! It seemed symbolic and fitting that somewhere deep in the woods on Vancouver Island, hanging from a tree branch, was that white swim suit, like a peace flag blowing in the wind.*

Chapter Eleven

My Awakening

WHO IS THE GREAT LOVE OF MY LIFE?
You may find when talking to your own girlfriends someday, Layla, that there is something about being needed by a man that keeps women occupied. Also remember, many men still think of women as possessions.

These days women have stepped out in front in some cases, and the men back them up—but that role is a hard sell for a man. *I prefer what my own grandmother told me and am passing it along to you, Layla.*

"The secret to a good relationship is choosing the right person, not just the first one, and always making the man believe that he thought of it, even if it was actually your original idea. If a man thinks it's his idea, even when it is actually what you wanted, they are much more likely to agree to it," she told me.

Wise woman, my grandmother, and she had a long and successful marriage, as did my own parents. *I realize now I should have listened to her more and not kept falling for the wrong man or missing the right one. Also it's okay to just be friends with a guy. It doesn't all have to be romantic, although it's easy to say in theory and harder to follow!*

What was I really looking for in life? Was I really finding it with Simon?

I've always been an artist, painter and photographer. Highly intuitive, and even when I made mistakes I believed in a higher power—things that we may not see but are there all the same. That helps me enjoy the beauty and mysteries that life offers, and create in whatever way I can. *The intellectuals I met were interesting, but why did I feel they were missing something?*

I was searching for something more than material and looked forward to going back, traveling again. I already knew I was not just a body or "hunk of meat"—that I had a mind and spirit. Simon threw me off track for a while there. He thought he already had all the answers and talked to me at length about the right and left brain. It was mostly a split brain theory, not a mental theory, of how the body reacted and how the right part of the brain controlled one side of the body and the left part of the brain the other side, but with his philosophical views thrown in. He said that meant one side of the brain was more creative and one more logical. But it ignored the fact that the imagination is not in a hunk of brain matter and it's actually simple to prove the "mind" is really not the brain. Of course Simon liked the theory since he is agnostic, and never believed in any God, or that the spirit lives on, or that there's a higher spiritual power at work at all. I think he expected me to think that, too, but I was trying to show him another view.

I already realized long before this that I was a soul with a mind and a body, and as a spirit could create ideas. Imagination was as crucial as intelligence and knowledge. *If you close your eyes and picture things you can tell. It was "me" as a spirit picturing things, not my eyes or my brain.*

A famous blind musician I met, Stevie Wonder, told me once when I was visiting an artist friend that he could actually "see" things and he was not dependent upon his eyes at all. *All those who have a good imagination seemed to know this.* But in my debates with Simon, he disagreed and had a way of pulling me into his point of view or not looking at another view. I felt both lucky to be an artist and lonely that he couldn't see my view too. I think I was always trying to get him to see another viewpoint and that was a mistake.

Sometimes people are just not able to see what you can, and that's okay. Keep your own counsel, Layla, and follow what is true for you.

Chapter Twelve

The Breakup Vow

I STILL LOVED SIMON, I REALLY DID. BUT AFTER A YEAR IN HALIFAX WITH him, something was missing, and I knew we had to break up. We both had trouble facing it. He was set in what he wanted to do. His life was under his strict control. After Nova Scotia, Simon was scheduled to teach philosophy at the University of Toronto. Toronto at that time was beginning to be a huge international city with a thriving arts community.

Simon was an enigma to me. He was mellow and relaxed on the one hand and rigid, opinionated on the other. He was always ready with a joint or a pint, but also fixed in his ideas about life. He was an avowed agnostic and didn't believe in anything he couldn't see or prove, but he liked a good challenge. He had to be right, and practiced this in debates with philosophy professors and students alike, always looking to win the argument, no matter what.

That was only one of many ways we were different.

He had done all he could for me, but now his help was holding me back from my own self-discoveries. Deep down I think Simon knew it too.

His last words were: "Whether it takes three months, three years or thirty years, we'll be together again sometime, somewhere." He said it sadly and deliberately as if meaning every word at the time.

"I believe it," I answered. I had to or the heartbreak at that moment would have been unbearable. We drank, smoked a little that night and made love so intensely we were sweating hard and exhausted, but nothing could dispel the feeling we had gone as far as we could together and now it was time to part.

"Where will you go?" I asked him.

"I'm going to stay at Francine's for now," Simon answered. I understood the only way he could leave me was to go to someone else—someone to comfort and support him throughout the break up.

"You can stay here," he said to me, since the room we had in the house on Palmerston Avenue owned by a philosophy professor was a large upstairs loft.

It was a great place and the price was right—one of those three-story skinny English houses with a small backyard. Also, I had a painting studio in the back with lots of light coming in. It was convenient to everything Toronto had to offer, close to Bloor and Young Streets near the heart of the city.

"Goodbye, Simon, I will never forget you and if it's right for both of us, we'll be together again." *I need to expand and learn for myself and then maybe find you again, if the love is still there*, I said to myself as we were holding back tears and embracing.

Emotion blanketed the room until the deep sorrow was just too much. I had to move, to get up. Simon's nerves were on edge like my own and the second he left I felt the vacuum immediately. However, what I discovered was that my own individual presence was intact. *"I" was still here and it was all right to be on my own without Simon,* I thought, suddenly awash in elation and relief.

Sometimes it can be scary on your own, Layla, but just remember you can be comfortable within yourself. Then you know you can survive anything.

But there was restlessness as well. I had to do something, find something that was still missing for me, something I had not quite defined yet. But I would know when I found it. That was when I decided to travel. But first I needed to work my buns off and make a ton of money to do that, never forgetting I was young and single. I guess you could say I wanted it all.

Landing a great job doing architectural renderings for a large engineering firm helped. The pay was about a thousand dollars a week—a lot of money in the mid seventies. I was saving, but also threw parties with artist friends and philosophy professors from the University of Toronto every other week for those few months on famous Palmerston Avenue. I had artists, musicians, dancers from the local troupes, and visiting musicians come to my parties—especially when I made bread and apple pies from scratch and had big blocks of cheese out on tables with lots of other food. *Hot fresh organic wheat bread and apple pie! Yum! I can still taste it.*

The alcohol was BYOB, bring your own bottle. I met people from all over the world and loved every minute of it. Toronto is known, by the way, as the New York of Canada, and that year it sure held that kind of intense excitement for me!

As an artist living in Toronto, now on my own, I kept busy painting and drawing. I took a large piece of silk and made a colorful batik painting in blues, greens, and deep reds using wax painted on the material to cover certain areas. Then I hand-painted a woman in the center balanced on a round globe, with arms stretched out. It turned out well and I hung it over the fireplace like a tapestry. There was also a professor who commissioned me to paint his wife, a friend of mine. He wanted a nude of her. After considering it for a while, I decided to paint her naked from a three-quarter view, looking out of an open attic window with light purple curtains flowing around her in the wind. Another painting was created in pastels and a third was acrylic on canvas. It was a ceiling painting of a solar system and nebula. I used a lot of black paint on that one, but the effect turned out well. There were other drawings and I even tried my hand at sculpture and pottery, getting into red clay, which felt squishy and felt a lot like making mud pies except on a potter's wheel. There was a definite technique to it. For me it was a productive time, except for the endless philosophic debates which I usually call "pointless arguing."

I remember one time when Simon and I were together, coming down the stairs and hearing the philosophy professors talking in our living room in Toronto. I got so frustrated with what they were spouting about Niechtze, Schopenhauer, and other philosophers that I said, "Why are you arguing about nothing? What practical value does it have in life? You talk about an endless bunch of old bullshit, from long dead men, that does no one any good! It may sound good to you, but how do you apply it now, to today's world?" They were a bit shocked, which for an Englishman means they paused and looked up at me with eyebrows slightly raised. Then they went on with their discussion.

Deep down, Simon may have realized some truth in what I was saying, as he had a slight smile, but he always had to save face with his "more intelligent than me" Oxford colleagues. I would describe the professors who came over as "arrogant, stuffy, and endlessly arguing about nothing really significant, but with an English accent.. Yet they were the first to applaud anything to do with sex and a party.

I felt for Simon, though, and saw something else in him, perhaps his ethical core, and loved him for that. But I realized something major was missing— something I needed spiritually and was determined to find out. I wanted to look into other views and had an urgency to explore them, learn from them, and to evolve, not just take what others taught as fact. My purpose in life was still urging me on from somewhere deep within. *How can I describe what I don't understand yet? For me I knew I had to do something, anything, to find out.*

Remember, when you were little and you thought you'd grow up and be a ballerina, princess, fireman or cowboy? Something cool, but you didn't know just what it was. Well, that was me, and I had to figure it out.

Going through my mind at the time was: *Who and where is the great love of my life?* Who is the man that really loves me for myself, and will stick around and help make it last? Someone to create with, who can open up to all the possibilities of a relationship and to all sides of himself with me, as well as let me open up too? And how do I decide between two men I care about whom both say they love and need me? Polygamy is illegal, I know. *So how do I choose?* Sometimes I really did care about two people at the same time, and it's hard to tell which relationship will last when you're in the thick of it.

In my naïve way, it always came down to *who needed me most.* At that time, I was innocent enough to believe that a guy lusting after me was the same as a guy needing me or sharing ourselves with each other including our viewpoints. This is not usually the case, though. *Young guys seem more governed by their hormones than girls. But for both, it's difficult to separate out feelings and emotions. Maybe that was why I gravitated to intellectuals; what they said fooled me into thinking they may have the answer. But they didn't, at least not for me.*

What did I really want? Time to find out.

Chapter Thirteen

Romancing through Europe

I NEED TO LET YOU KNOW, MY LAYLA, HOW I ENDED UP IN EUROPE AND *then in Nepal, of all places. It started when I traveled abroad the first time and now I felt that itch to travel again.* Simon was still on my mind and I couldn't seem to shake him. I was saving up enough money to escape again.

With enough money in my pocket and bags packed, I hopped a plane headed overseas. The first time I had the opportunity to go to London on an art scholarship but now I was returning to Europe on my own!

Maybe I should have stayed in London on scholarship the previous months before this, but now I was ready to see the rest of Europe and jumped at the chance to do so. After landing and visiting friends in England, two of them wanted me to join them in going across the English Channel to Paris on the hovercraft. I immediately decided to go. The boat skimmed on the top of the waves, and sped us to France in an hour or so. I had grown up with boats at the lake and loved the wind and sea spray shooting out behind us like geysers as we sped along from island to mainland.

My good friends, Neal and Giselle (who was Parisian) helped to make the time magical. Giselle was a thin, brown-haired beauty and her boyfriend Neal was a tall, dark-haired Englishman. They were a good match and looked happy together. They took me everywhere. Paris museums and buildings are enchanting, with art from the 1890s and 1920s, some of my favorite eras. The Monet, Rembrandt and Gauguin paintings seen up close are incomparable. Having the opportunity to view them, see every brushstroke, the depth of the paint, the texture created, and the composition of light and darks gifted me with the best kind of education. *Wait 'til you see it for yourself, Layla!*

And, then, there was Paris itself. The people walking along the avenues dressed so artfully, streets with cobblestones, old stone buildings with ornate patterns up top with immortal gargoyles peering down at the tiny people walking on the sidewalks below. The river Seine and ancient bridges crossing it led to the round-about, where taxis mindlessly sped through taking one of the roads that were like spokes in a gigantic wheel. The tall Eiffel Tower was handy to use as a compass point to tell where you were in the city. All the delicious smells of superb pastries and coffee from the outdoor cafes that wafted over the city—I took it all in.

Yes, the Paris atmosphere is delightful; the palaces and museums are regal and the food chic, but the real Paris for me was getting into the underground clubs that my friends knew about. Listening to African drums, dancing, and seeing the wild exotic performers was the crowning experience. This total immersion in the city around me helped make the language difference no problem at all. I knew I would never see something like this on the usual tourist trip, nothing like this back home, and needed to make the most of it.

That was where I met Joachim. He was Paris to me, and we had a whirlwind romance. He was a native and, with my friends, showed me the backside of Paris, where the streets were not so clean and buildings were in need of repair, but where the music inside was exciting. Also he seemed to wash his hands at least ten times a day and always had to be so clean. *What was that all about?* I think he was being cautious and had a bad experience, maybe with a past girlfriend or relative. *A definite phobia about cleanliness!* He gave me a picture of himself and knew I was going to be leaving. It was his way of saying "remember me."

It helped to have someone translate to make the language difference not too difficult. Instinctively I could tell from the speaker's tone of voice if I was being complimented or insulted in French. It was a time when Americans were more welcome, but still if you didn't speak French you were considered somewhat savage. But no matter what the language, some things don't need translation like swearing, for instance. Or love. You can always tell when someone is giving you a compliment or cursing at you, even if you don't know the language at all.

And the men were very smooth, their voices almost musical. Young French men were cocky just like men all over the world, and I didn't mind the way they tried to pick me up because, of course, the language lent itself to seduction even if I didn't fully understand it. *I felt free to be seduced by Paris itself more than by any man, however, and reveled in just being myself.*

Chapter Fourteen

Terrifying Times

FROM PARIS I LEFT NEAL, GISELLE, AND JOACHIM, DETERMINED TO hitchhike to Italy. I had made friends with some Italians while in Toronto and wanted to visit them in Firenze ("Florence"). *I have to say, Layla, in truth everything wasn't always a joy. There were scary situations I found myself in when going through Europe on my own.* Just going through Europe as a single young girl can be very dangerous, especially when I hitchhiked. A bit oblivious to this, I was fearless, being so young. It was touch-and-go each time in a dangerous situation. *Reflecting on it later I know if I had hesitated and handled it differently it's possible I would not be here with you now, my love.*

I hopped onto the passenger seat of a large semi-truck traveling through France south to Italy. The driver was a simple truck driver, middle aged, non-descript with a scruffy beard. He didn't look threatening at all and spoke a little English. I spoke little French, but we mimed and gestured a lot to make ourselves understood. He seemed reserved and I thought maybe he just wanted some company on a long road trip. Hitchhiking as a student was sometimes the only way to get around and very popular at the time.

The cities and countryside flew by, and off in the distance I occasionally saw a castle or very old stone structure—perhaps a church. The grass was very green, and crops of trees dotted the countryside with farmhouses and animals appearing among the endless grape vines. It seemed so much more ancient here compared to America. There so much more history to every old building and I couldn't believe some were still standing after hundreds of years. I was tempted to stop along the way and see some of the beautiful older villages; some of them without much change in many generations. This was so much a part of European landscape, I wanted to get my sketchpad out and paint it all. I see now what moved the Old Masters to pull out their linen canvases and easels.

There is a little known fact about truck stops. Truckers everywhere know truck stops that have the best food for the least amount of money. We stopped for lunch in an out-of-the way small restaurant—which had a small living quarter in the back. The wine they served was probably from a local vineyard and the flavor was not too sweet, not too bitter, but just right! I vowed to find out more about wines upon my return to the States, but I felt sure that those in France were superior to anything I tasted before.

The afternoon truck stop meal was made up of the most delicious soup with meat served with fresh bread. The wine, bottled locally, was served as part of the meal to teenagers as well as adults. I have no idea what it was called, but fell in love with French country food right then and there. My head was spinning a bit when we hit the road again, and I looked at the driver to make sure he was sober. *Well, at least he could stand up.*

It was getting late as we traveled along talking less and less, watching the countryside whizzing by. Coming into Lyon, a town in the south of France which had a train station, I could see the shadows from the setting sun and felt queasy for some reason. The train was supposed to stop in Lyon, near the Italian border and going on to Italy, so this was the end of my ride.

I looked over at the French truck driver with his scruffy beard, thinning hair, with blue-collar clothes on and saw he had a harsh look in his eye. He was silent most of the trip, and after the café lunch he did look a little inebriated.

Suddenly he was leaning over and grabbing me. He was slowing down and I knew his intention was to stop and jump me. His gritty hands were reaching everywhere. It was dark out, hard to see, and I knew it could easily turn ugly. *Maybe he felt I owed him something?* I sensed something was about to happen, and my survival instincts took over.

I shouted, "NO!!!" very loudly and suddenly swung my heavy backpack at him, clobbering him with it while turning the handle of the passenger door. I just had time to open my door quickly and jump/fall down from the passenger side at the same time. Jumping out of the truck was not an easy task from the height of a big semi-truck still moving, and I stumbled to the ground. Then he stopped the truck and I heard the driver's door scraping open. The trucker was getting out on his side to follow me and I knew my life depended upon the next few seconds.

Were we near enough to the train station. My heart pounding in my ears was so loud I couldn't think. *Where was it? How far away? Can I make it?* I was so scared he would catch up to me shortly and attack me before I had a chance to escape. It spurred me on and I ran faster.

Remember people in accidents doing superhuman things, I thought to myself. I can do this! I ran faster and faster—so fast I think I broke a track record!Before I touched ground and took off running for the train station, I had desperately hoped it wasn't too far away and I could escape. But now I heard the clack, clack, clack of footsteps behind me on the street. Turning, I saw a shadow running toward me. The footsteps sounded so loud to me, I wondered if he was right behind ready to pounce. *Was I going to make it now?* I kept running.

After what seemed like an eternity, I saw the glow of train station lights ahead, and some people milling around in the distance. *If only I could get out of the dark and into the wash of street lights, someone would surely see me.*

*One, two, three, four…*I counted every step to freedom. My heart was beating faster than my feet could catch up, but I noticed every step I took was getting further and further away from my attacker. There it was just ahead. Fortunately I was a fast runner or I don't know what would have happened. Shaking when I made it to the train station lights, I had no more breath left to scream or even talk. But I made it!

The train was going where I wanted to go, passing Switzerland on the way to Italy. Paying and jumping aboard, I glanced behind me and for the first time felt safe again.

Chapter Fifteen

In Love with Italy

Next thing I knew, I was riding the train from France to Rome, the capital of the Holy Roman Empire for thousands of years. The saying "All roads lead to Rome" took on new meaning for me. I got to see the usual tourist places in one whirlwind day, wondering how a great civilization could fall like it had.

The Coliseum was in ruins, but I could actually feel the way it must have been—thousands of people on stone tiers going up to the top, looking down into the round central staging area. The gladiators fighting the animals and each other with poor victims released to the lions, all going on with deafening cheers from the crowd of spectators in togas and jewelry. I was momentarily stunned by the picture that the site brought to mind. Barbaric and yet mesmerizing at the same time. *Is this like our fascination for highway accidents?* I thought. *Or extreme sporting events, smashing into cars or beating people up? It was daunting to imagine.* I guess our love of spectacles doesn't go out of style, no matter what the generation or epoch.

But my intention was to get to Florence. I had studied Michelangelo in art college and his statue of *David* which stood over seventeen-feet high in the Galleria dell Academia, had caught the imagination of Italians at the time as well as people all over the world thereafter. I loved all his paintings, too, with their vibrant colors and perspective. He was a big influence on me. I just had to see *David* for myself.

When I walked into the museum, the statue was under a domed roof, in a special area. *The theme of a giant against a country boy with a sling shot is inspiring,* I thought as I stood looking at the intricate work. My first glimpse of *David* gave me chills up and down my back and tears rushed unbidden to my eyes. The statue seemed so *alive,* the way it was lit, with the pearly white Carrara marble that looked almost translucent so you could see every muscle outlined and sculpted to perfection. I really wondered if he moved after a while and stood in awe examining every inch.

The old stone buildings, stone statues and magnificent artwork were even better seen from the rooftop of my friend's Florence apartment building as the sun set over the tops of the sculptured landscape of this great city.

How can anyone not love Florence?" I thought, as the pink sunset glinted off stone, glass, ceramic tiles, tops of sculptures, and ornate old buildings. There was something about the light; warm and pink, giving a slight glow to everything it touched. Mario, who owned the flat we were staying in, was a young, good-looking Italian friend of a Toronto buddy I knew. He was with his Italian friends and we all raised our glasses, drank to the sunset and to art in general, silent a moment, each of us in our own private thoughts.

From living in Toronto I had met so many people from other countries during parties and events that I had a slew of invitations to visit them and their counterparts when in Europe. *Halleluiah!* That was how I found out about Mario in Italy. I couldn't afford to do the tourist thing; staying in hotels and so on. Plus I wanted to stop and paint along my travels. So instead I stayed with friends all along the way, paid for some of the food and shared stories about America or my own experiences with them as they shared knowledge of their country with me. *Perfect exchange.* Immersing myself in the culture—this was an artist's dream and proved to be one of the most vital things about my travels.

Chapter Sixteen

Never a Tourist

W HEN YOU GET TO SEE IT YOURSELF, MY LAYLA, REMEMBER THE SECRET *of Florence is the fact that if you go up on the rooftops you have the best view of the city and can see some of the tops of sculptures and artistically decorated buildings all laid out before you during sunset.*

Eating a meal of soup and fresh breads, wine and Italian coffee with my Italian friends, we watched the sun go down with a sigh over the golden and pink beauty before us. It was spectacular, and the meal tasted all that much better, with lots of our laughter ringing out above the city noises.

The Italians liked to tease me about traveling alone and had a lively curiosity about Americans.

"Do you have places like this in America?" Mario and the others asked. "What was it like traveling by yourself?"or "Did your boyfriend abandon you?" or "Did your parents really let you come over on your own?" or even "You must be a rich American if you can travel around like this."

"No, not at all. I made all my own money. I'm an artist too. But I had to see Italy; it's where it all started. The Renaissance—with Lorenzo Di Medici, Patron of the Arts, who called upon artists and scientists from all civilized countries to come to Florence. It was a magical time," I said with a smile.

My friends were full of enthusiasm and uninhibited in their communication and attitudes. I instantly caught the spirit. They used their hands to talk, so it was actually easier to understand Italian, but I liked to communicate through art. I always think of this as the "Italian Way."

Taking out my pastels and art pad the next day, I did a drawing of Mario when we traveled into the country to swim, actually to go skinny dipping in one of the waterfall pools. He was naked, like all of us. I captured him from the back from a three-quarter view, sitting cross-legged on the ground. He was lit from behind looking like he was in contemplation in a yoga position but he wasn't. This was just after the pretzel of our entangled bodies went sliding down the slick mossy rocks of the small falls from above, laughing all the way down. We ended up in the pool of spring water so clear you could drink it. It was hot out, the water felt good as we splashed each other with a vengeance, cooling each of us off as we finally dropped down on the grass exhausted.

What fun! *Just what I needed, our own "swimming hole" I thought to myself.* And the countryside was charming. No wonder people want to visit Italy more than any other country in Europe.

It was then that I decided to go visit my friends, Dmitri and his wife, in Greece since they begged me to stop by. After all, it was right next door!

To get to Athens I had to take a train down to Naples which went across the east side of Italy to the coast. While traveling through Italy, I was enchanted looking at scenes that could have been from a fairy tale. It was all right there, whirling by, just beyond me. From there I took a ferry to Athens, going past some beautiful islands on the way.

I could feel my next adventure was about to begin, and I was full of hope, happy after my Italian experience and what I would discover next. *I wonder where Simon is now,* I remember thinking fleetingly.

Meditating upon the Italian countryside

Chapter Seventeen

Naples Night Fright

ICAME INTO THE NAPLES STATION AT 3:00 A.M. AND TO BE HONEST IT WAS a little scary being all alone. At this late hour, I started imagining scenes from *The Godfather* and tried to shake the feeling of foreboding.

Looking out the train window in the dark as we stopped, I saw only shadows of people slipping away quickly into the night like wraiths. It made me wish the train had kept going. I let out a weary sigh when I found out it was stopped here until the next morning. I had nowhere to go. Exhausted from traveling and disheartened when I heard this train would not be taking off until 6:00 a.m., I decided to curl up on the empty train on a cushioned seat. I had my ticket and found I had the right train leaving in the morning, so decided to stay put.

The lighting was dim and seats were long enough to stretch out on. With no one around it seemed like a good temporary bed to me. I settled down lengthwise on the seat with my feet up and head down on a cushion to see if I could catch a nap. Immediately I started drifting off, remembering a dream.

I was on a large bed and it was falling slowly in black space. I could see the stars around me as I flew downward on my bed like a magic carpet ride, gently turning while falling through endless space, never hitting the bottom. This was a reoccurring dream.

Suddenly, I sat up in the seat, wide awake. Something was wrong...

I sensed the presence of someone there in the train car with me. It was like a waking dream, and at first I didn't know what was happening. I sensed breathing, heavy breathing, then the stale smells of tobacco mixed with some kind of spices in the air. Finally I heard the noises of shuffling boots and a cough. *Was I still dreaming?*

When I felt a hand reach out and touch me, my adrenals kicked in and I jumped up in one fast motion. *NO!* Even in the dim light I caught sight of one of the train employees (*a conductor*, I thought) and saw him coming straight for me. He reached out trying to grope me. I vaguely saw he was an older man, just a skinny shadow, with dark hair and even darker eyes glowering in the dark. I was on full alert now. He reached out to grab me, to grope me, to hurt me, and I was so frightened everything seemed to be in slow motion.

Time stretched to encompass my stopped heart, but in the next moment it began to beat again. Faster and faster, the blood was flowing through me.

Now, I could smell his breath on me. *Disgusting!*

He came closer and I pulled away. I saw then he was in a dark uniform, had a scruffy beard, smelled of cigarettes, was short of stature but looked very intent with a dangerous gleam in his eyes.

This was real! *I had to do something, quick!*

My trusty backpack, solid as a rock with its metal frame, once more came to my rescue. I slammed the backpack into my potential rapist hard and then took off running out the door down to the end of the station. He had fallen down, but I knew he would be up and chasing me. *I only had a short lead. Would it be enough?*

No, Not again! I thought as I ran almost out of breath for the station.

There were lots of lights ahead and a few people. This time they were much closer and I was determined to make it. Thinking and talking out loud to myself while moving, "*Shit, shit, shit! I am not going to be a victim. I can do this!*"

I ran so fast I didn't take a second to look back until I was there. Surrounded by a few people, I doubled over panting hard to catch my breath. The light just ahead shed its beams exposing the dark recesses in the station and the darker recesses of human frailty. The conductor had vanished.

I wondered if I had knocked some sense into him, made him reevaluate his actions. *Good! Well, that's one train worker that won't be molesting girls tonight!* I started to get my balance back—in disgust and anger, far better than the gripping fear I felt a moment ago.

My relief after being so very afraid came out as laughter, and I was laughing so hard I bent down to suck in breath, then starting coughing with tears in my eyes. After looking around at the few concerned people staring at me, it didn't seem scary anymore. After all "how bad can it be" with the Naples train crew right around the corner, but at the time I almost peed my pants I was so frightened. *That would have been the ultimate embarrassment!*

Lucky for me I kept in good shape hiking. I don't want to think about what could have happened in that secluded train car at 3:00 a.m. in that lonely Naples station. Still a little shaky thinking about it, I spent the rest of the time trying to calm down, sitting on a bench with several others waiting for the train—just breathing in and out, in and out—sleep was all but forgotten.

While I'm sure that in the light of day Naples can be a friendly place, it was never the same for me after that.

Time to move on.My friends were waiting for me.

Chapter Eighteen

Greek Gods and Other Delights

I found my Greek friends' small but well-decorated home in Athens very charming. They gave me a room as my base when in Greece and were impeccable hosts, asking me any news about Canada and sharing stories with me. Then I went over by ferry to skin dive off the island of Crete, recommended by my friend Dmitri. While walking through a canyon full of ancient ruins I imagined how Greece used to be.

You may see it too, in your mind's eye, my curious Layla, with stunnin. stone pillars and a feeling of history in the air, as if men in togas would suddenly appear animatedly discussing the wisdom of Socrates or Plato with great passion. Truth be told, that wisdom was a civilizing force for the world from then onward.

When in Greece you have to dance in a Greek restaurant at least once, and I loved the enthusiasm of the Greek people I met. Working to get the steps down, I realized it was a simple dance and after a while it was second nature and I really started to get the hang of it, enjoying the dancing. The fun had begun again and the scary times were almost forgotten. Dancing was the best therapy.

Seeing the haunted ruins of the Acropolis awash with colored lights by night, I could imagine the Senate of long ago meeting on the steps discussing the beginnings of the first Olympic Games or a principle of government. But afterwards I was in for more fun. Going to the seashore by day and meeting a handsome young man, Nikos, seemed part of the enchantment. Being wooed by Nikos, fair-haired and fearless, whose father happened to be a descendent of a famous Greek general—all in all, it was a pretty normal whirlwind week.

Nikos professed his love, and asked to come with me on my travels, but I realized his powerful family may not like that arrangement and had visions of them sending the Greek Army after us like something out of the Trojan War! He gave me his picture and vowed to come see me in America instead. Kissing me tenderly, he whispered how much he loved me and held me close, which was so romantic I could hardly stand it. I wavered and almost took him with me. *Should I get a trunk and take him back with me? Probably too risky!*

In Athens I got word that Simon was going to Nepal to visit Terry and Mary, friends of his whom I had met in London. They were interns (doctor and nurse) volunteering up in the hills of Nepal with a charity. It sounded like an exotic place full of Lamas, and I imagined chanting monks and magical experiences, so Nepal struck me as the place to go next. I suddenly decided I needed to be there. Simon was there after all, and something may have changed by now. I was still searching, looking for answers to questions about life and love and maybe, just maybe I would find them in Nepal.

My next step was going through Yugoslavia by train from Athens to get to Frankfurt, Germany, and catch a plane. The flight in Germany was very cheap for students like me going to New Delphi, India. My destination was Nepal, but to get there I had to go to India first and cross the border. *On to India it was then!*

Before when I thought of India, I saw some exotic land of sun with elephants, monkeys, and tigers in the jungle, with everyone in bright colors. Something out of the *Jungle Book* mixed up with the Taj Mahal and Bollywood images.

It couldn't have been further from the truth.

Chapter Nineteen

Culture Shock

INDIA WAS A SHORT PLANE RIDE AWAY, SO WHY NOT? I THOUGHT AS I imagined seeing Simon again. The plane took off the next day in Germany and I was on the student discount flight to India. Nepal was only a short bus ride through the mountain pass from India after that.

There I was, walking through the streets of New Delhi with other students, about five of them from America led by a guy named Michael, humming "*In a god-da da-vee-da ba-by*" in a hundred degree heat at sunrise. I just came from the airport and I swear it felt like I landed in another solar system!

They call it "culture shock" and that's exactly how I felt at the time. A shock to see people in such different conditions, talking and thinking differently; people dressed in simple or shabby garb but most women in saris and with red dots on the center of their foreheads. *I had to find out what that was all about.* I saw an older man with a scruffy beard and a turban on his head praying at a little shrine with flowers and incense, set up to honor Hindu gods. *Was it dedicated to Shiva or Krishna?* The people looked so thin and the streets so dirty. The few Tibetan monks I saw had golden or red robes from Dharmsala up in northern India and had shaved heads. I could picture them in their temple, chanting as they sat cross legged with a big brass gong clanging, calling them to prayer.

You may someday go to a third world country, Layla, and see the same things I saw, but much worse. It's an education of sorts and definitely makes you appreciate how much you have.

I needed to acclimate to this very foreign land as fast as possible if I was going to understand it.

The streets were full of vendors selling anything you can think of, mixed up among all the poverty and degradation. It's such an entirely different culture from where I came. The shock was worse because I didn't have any preparation beforehand. Shocked at the poverty I saw around me, the first sight was of dirty rags of muted colors on brown skin, children running in the streets without an arm, or hobbling along missing a leg with a bloody stump. It was like one big outdoor emergency field hospital but without the doctors! Their sewer seemed to be the ditch running along each street, smelling disgusting, with beggars, merchants, and families squatting on sidewalks nearby. Other foreigners had the same dazed look that I had. It was dirty and smelly but people seemed to ignore it and get along.

At first all I could think of was where is the bathroom? Possibly that gutter I just saw with brown liquid flowing down the street was it! I was a little alarmed not having modern conveniences but assumed once I got to our hostel it would be fine. But, the youth hostels had a primitive bathroom in one section of the room with a partition around it. The toilet was a hole in the cement or stone floor that you squatted over, and it doubled as a shower drain with a metal water spigot up about breast-high for me! *Well, nothing like roughing it*! I decided to consider this camping out, and not to assume any modern conveniences would be available. It helped me remain calm.

There were the overpowering mix of smells that suffused the air, the smells of garam masala spice, human bodies, misery and motion, along with the feeling of wonder that started to permeate my consciousness as I walked along the streets carrying my backpack over my shoulder. The food I finally got a chance to eat was delicious. Chickens freshly killed in the backyard with Indian spices accompanied by bowls of vegetables I didn't know the name of served with fluffy rice. They prepared small bowls of vegetables covered with different sauces which you could mix into your larger rice bowl. The food was always spicy and I wasn't used to that kind of hot food. It definitely took some getting used to!

I joined four other students who were going into one of the better restaurants just to get out of the heat. When the server brought the meal, I found out how hot Indian food really is.

"Try this," one of the students I think was named Michael told me passing over a plate of food, "but watch out for the peppers!" he added too late.

I immediately opened my mouth of food moaning, "*Ouch! Wow, it's too hot, it's too spicy!*" as tears streamed freely down my face. It was at least a half hour before I could feel my tongue again. The students were howling with laughter and the waiters were trying to keep a straight face. *Well at least the other students got a kick out of it.*

Tall stone buildings dominated in the main city, ancient and crumbling even before my country was founded, and interesting to me with several very different architectural themes from ornate to pristine. They ranged from cut stone to rock-cut structures in caves then to wooden and now steel reinforced modern buildings. Most of the larger buildings are Hindu or Buddhist temples or stupas and some Muslim architecture like the Taj Mahal. The first city to thrive in India actually existed in northern India in 2,500 B.C. and had large stone walls, bath houses, warehouses, and paved streets.

But I was looking forward to Nepal and wondered what Simon was doing there right now. I was trying to absorb all I could of the Indian culture, but in my heart I was racing to Nepal.

Chapter Twenty

More about India: Mysterious and Exotic

T HE FEELING OF FAMILIARITY KEPT HITTING ME AS I TRAVELED. The people inhabiting this region from India to Nepal, both the living as well as those of the past alike, permeated the area with their thoughts and beliefs and if you are very perceptive you can actually feel it.

It feels so different here, Layla—not the scenery, or the physical manifestations, but something else impossible to explain in words. It hit me like a shock wave when I emerged from the plane in New Delphi, but now I quickly realized the real shock was about the Indian people's beliefs.

A combination of things intrigued me—the people's beliefs that they live on and have lived before in other forms, the spiritual side of reincarnation, and the Buddhist values of peace and serenity, all had an effect on me. Even the vast poor, living on the streets, didn't seem threatening at all—just disturbing. It shook up my beliefs and middle class values; especially our striving for more material things. They had so very little here but seemed at peace.

The people in India believe that what you do in this life affects what happens in the next. This may very well be true, Layla. Many people believe this. Their attention is more on the future and the search for enlightenment rather than on war or the buck, but to be honest they also worried how they were going to make their next meal! I found out, over and over, that they have the viewpoint that humans are not just a hunk of meat but a spiritual entity animating the body and that the spirit lives on. It made me pause. *When you do immoral or unethical things in this life, will that carry over into the next life?* I wondered.

It's also a very good reason to treat others as you would want to be treated, which is also a Christian concept. They believe we are all immortal to some degree—*going on and on to I know not where,* as one of my favorite poems said so well. It struck a chord within me, begging the question *"Who or what are we anyhow?"*

I needed to explore more of this unusual culture and the best way for me was to visit their artists but after I drag my body back to the youth hostel for some much needed sleep!

Chapter Twenty-One

Garments and Sitars

WHEN I WOKE UP WITH A START IN THE YOUTH HOSTEL THE NEXT DAY, I decided it was time to explore. I was already sweating from the heat and it was going to be a few days before heading to Nepal, time enough to go to the garment district I heard so much about. The artists there weave material into the most gorgeous cloth—mostly cotton and silk—and also employ artists to create Batik designs on the material. This process uses wax and colored dyes artistically to make interesting or traditional patterns but all very colorful.

Many of the bolts of material I saw were created for saris—a dress-like garment created by a continuous length of cloth wrapped precisely to create a skirt and a top with a piece of material used like a cape over the shoulder. Yes, saris are made out of one piece of cloth, folded and wrapped and not cut into pattern.

I was amazed when the women showed me how to drape a sari, folding it, tucking it in, and wrapping the material to create an effect of elegance in a long dress. I couldn't help myself and bought a beautiful length of silk, enough for a sari, pale blue with maroon designs. When I put it on, I felt like a present all wrapped up for Christmas in sensuous silk!

I could really see why they wear them. They're very comfortable and elegant. It never again seemed strange to see a woman dressed in a sari.

There was music coming from another shop nearby, and I discovered someone playing a sitar. His playing brought back memories of hearing Ravi Shankar play. I'm not one of those "impulse buy" girls, but I couldn't resist buying a sitar after I strummed a few notes. *I played piano for five years, so how hard could a sitar be?* The sound is so unusual, like an exotic guitar so I thought *why not bring back a little of India with me?!* I forgot all about how inconvenient it would be traveling with a large sitar. I had abandoned all practicality for the moment. Music is magical.

I strummed my sitar and hummed along to music only I could hear.

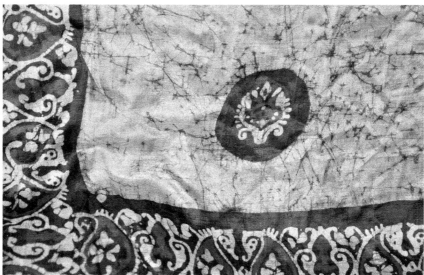

Batik patterns on silk

Chapter Twenty-Two

The Ganges Funeral Pyre

THE SMOKE WISPS AND FIRE LOOKED LIKE THEY CAME STRAIGHT OUT of the water, dead ahead.

On the way across India to reach Nepal from New Delhi, I took a train to the Ganges River. Some of the students I was with took a boat ride down the Ganges, but I decided not to join them. I was more curious about the stories I had heard about how the Indian people, the Hindus, handle their dead. I wanted to see if these stories were true, so I walked over to a shallow place in the river where people could wade into the water. They cremate bodies next to the river.

I was surprised to see a couple of people in the water toting what looked like a long floating body. They seemed to be praying over it. Then one of them lifted the floating body while another one wrapped it with linen. The wet linen was clinging to the body. They lifted it out of the water and very reverently took it up on shore. These were dead people, dead bodies with no spirit around them anymore and it was believed that the Ganges, a sacred river, blessed the dead for their journey into the next life.

Just then it reminded me of the fact that a billion or two people (Hindu, Buddhist, Shinto and even early Christians) on this earth believe in past and future lives and reincarnation.

Actually, now that I thought about it, that would explain a lot about how people act, maybe acting out something from another life, I thought. *You may see examples of this in your own life, Layla.*

They believe and acknowledge that the spirit lives on, and can then inhabit another new body after this body is worn out and dies. *Well, Why not?* It explains a lot of things, such as why I can feel I knew someone before, even if I've just met the person. It clarifies why I feel I've done a similar action before.

You know that déjà vu feeling you get sometimes, Layla? That may just be remembering a time that really happened somewhere before now.

The Nepalese and Tibetans believe your spirit lives on in another human body and another life, if you've been "good." (Otherwise you may end up as a cockroach next time!) They believe the "you" that is your core, your essence, keeps going. Or, to put it more accurately, that essence, your soul, is immortal.

I know most people I have talked to all over the world do believe in a higher power and their concept of God varies. As the Hindus and Buddhists explained it, they are not just flesh and blood, and really feel they are a spirit, a soul or essence that animates their body.

Anyway, when I saw those dead bodies in the Ganges, it was so obvious that there was no one home. The souls were gone.

I looked over on my left and saw them placing a body on a platform of a huge pile of wood and knew I was witnessing a funeral pyre. Another stack of wood was next to the platform where the linen-wrapped body rested atop of the pile of wood. As I watched, someone with a torch lit the pile underneath the body. With a whoosh everything was on fire! People who loved them, friends and family, stood around saying a few words. Some were crying while others looked on with a pail of water at their side. They were ready to put out the fire when it became too hot or went on too long, as everyone stood on the banks of the Ganges.

I remembered seeing pictures of the Viking funeral, being from Swedish and Dutch ancestors, and this one on the banks of the River Ganges looked like a Viking funeral without the ship. What a powerful way to go! Fire and smoke until all becomes ashes that will then get absorbed back to earth again. It seemed much more logical than putting a decaying dead body into a box in the ground. There are much better ways to remember loved ones than visiting graves where usually no spirit still lives.

I suddenly recalled when I was seventeen being in a huge church. Walking slowly up to a casket, I was a bit nervous, somewhat scared, and then I looked inside and saw the painted face and body of my dead grandfather in repose. This was not the same person at all that I remember. I was the very last person to see him alive. He was taken by a nerve disease where he couldn't speak, but communicated by squeezing my hand. He was so alive then, but now he really wasn't around. I caught myself thinking, "That's not my grandfather. Where is he now?"

My attention returned to the huge funeral pyre with flames licking the air. It was jarring and I knew that I would never look at an open casket and graveside at a western funeral the same way again.

Chapter Twenty-Three

Kingdom of Nepal

AFTER THE GANGES, I HOPPED THE BUS THAT WAS GOING TO NEPAL through the mountain pass from India—the one on which I charmed the driver to let me ride on top with the backpacks. *This was the beginning of my experience in Nepal, Layla, as I told you before when you asked how I felt coming through the mountain pass for the first time, riding on backpacks on the very top of the old bus. It was the ride of my life!*

Nothing blocked my exotic views. New sights, sounds, people, scenery, and landscapes going swiftly by. Taking it all in, I had a fleeting feeling I had been here before…maybe a long, long time ago, in another lifetime perhaps…or someplace similar, very long ago.

At this moment in time, in this particular place on the planet, I was overcome by an incredibly strong feeling that I was *exactly* where I needed to be. Also I knew I was on an adventure in life where every turn in the road, every step along the way, led to somewhere I was searching to find—just ahead, out of reach. *Each person along the way was there for some reason, to complete an experience that had its roots in the purpose for my search. And each person mattered and made a difference in my search. Whether they were someone to talk to, take comfort from, fool me, make me stronger, or give me hope.*

At the same time, underneath it all were yearnings for love and real purpose in my life. To gain this, I needed knowledge. In traveling I hoped that I would learn from what was happening and from the people around me. I was immersing myself in life. Even the difficulties, the hurts that made me pull away at first, did not deter me from going right back into it, right back into life in all its forms.

For how do you test out your perceptions, your ideas, Layla? If you don't try it out, if you don't do it, you won't have the certainty.

So here I was, following my perceptions and searching for my own truth despite all the wrong detours of the past. For eventually I knew I would find it and it would set me free. I just knew.

"Beep, beep!" the honking of the bus shocked me out of my reverie and signaled another car passing with the hills streaking on either side of us. *Hang on tight!* I thought to myself as we barely missed hitting the car.

A thought rushed in from a remembered poem that goes,

> *"This is thy hour O Soul,*
> *Thy free flight into the wordless time and space,*
> *Away from books, away from art, the day erased, the lesson done.*
> *Thee, fully forth emerging, silent, gazing,*
> *Pondering the themes thou lovest best.*
> *Night, sleep, and the stars."*
> By Walt Whitman© [1]

As we flew along on the bus passing into Nepal, a mist swirled around us. Entering the Kathmandu Valley, the mist lifted showing the panorama before us. The magical kingdom spread out before us like a wave of a wand.

I was tired and hungry when I jumped off the bus along with several other students and "tourists." I didn't pay much attention to my fellow travelers, all men, at first. We were too busy looking at the sights.

When I arrived at the Kathmandu youth hostel, I immediately made friends, most of them European—especially the boy from Switzerland, Michel. It was a bit of home since most everyone spoke English, so I was less homesick. I was over six thousand miles away and half way around the world from my own home, but quickly got caught up in the mystery and magic of Nepal and had no time to miss people. I always felt if you carried the people you loved inside you, in your thoughts, you could never really lose them. As it was, I was too busy seeing new sights, hearing new sounds,

---

1 Whitman, Walt. *Leaves of Grass.* Philadelphia: David McKay, [c1900]; Bartleby.com, 1999. "A Clear Midnight," pg. 487

smelling new things completely foreign and exotic from my hometown in Minnesota.

Later on I found that one of them, my friendly Swiss friend, Michel, had a car, a French-made Citroen. I could hardly believe it when he told me he had driven the car all the way overland from Switzerland! He wanted me to join him and some other European friends to go eat. I made friends with this group of students, never imagining what was in store for me next.

I found out about their spices the hard way. Nepalese food used garam masala (a blend of cumin, turmeric, cardamom, coriander, cinnamon, cloves, bay leaves, ginger and nutmeg in a delicious combination!) in sauces with vegetables and fresh meat. It came in small bronze bowls along with a large bowl of rice. The procedure for eating is as follows: wash your hands first in a bowl of warm water, then taking the smaller bowls of vegetables and meat, use your hands to scoop the food into the larger rice bowl. Mix it or not, then using your fingers and hand, push the food to the rim of the bowl and into your mouth! Eating this way went fast—all with bare hands and without silverware. Then afterwards, the process includes washing your hands in a bowl of water again and wiping them on a cloth. Apparently, no one got sick from this, so I dug in! *When in Rome, right?*

It was my art and willingness to communicate that granted me access to people of all varieties and to their inner stories, Layla. But you may notice that the choice of Nepal to visit made it instantly a challenge to understand and adapt.

Statue of the Monkey God

Chapter Twenty-Four

Patron of the Arts

IF ART OPENS DOORS, TRAVEL OPENS THE MIND, AND BECAUSE I WAS willing to experience anything, I was given the gift of meeting a definite VIP in Nepal, someone who gave me the best insight into this magical country of Nepal. *Maybe it was not by chance that we met.*

Michel's Citroen had made it all the way from Switzerland so we all thought, *what the heck*, it was probably safe to drive it around Kathmandu and see some of the sights. I was fortunate to be staying in the same youth hostel as Michel and he drove me around. Everything I saw was so different from Minnesota or Wisconsin, yet the people here were kind too. They liked to bargain in the open-air markets and were especially curious about American students and the young people visiting from Europe.

I immediately liked them, Layla, and I bet you would too. The Nepalese have a happy disposition and like to communicate even if I couldn't quite understand everything. They could always make the motions and gestures to get their point across and so did I.

"What do you do back in the States?" Michel asked me.

"I'm an artist, and recently got a scholarship to go to England as an exchange student last year, but took some time off now," I told him.

Upon learning I was a painter, he immediately wanted me to meet someone.

"You have to come with me and meet George," he said, excited. "He supports artists.. (He pronounced George, "gay-og" the Austrian way.)

85

"I met this Patron of the Arts, you could call him," he went on to tell me, speaking accented English, "and he's a European from Austria, who is writing a book. In Kathmandu, he has a whole house full of artists that are helping him with his book. He's looking for someone who draws and can paint to illustrate some of his book. Why don't you come along with me and meet him?"

I then told Michel about my art training and more about my scholarship to the London Art College. I also showed Michel a couple of my sketches on my drawing pad and he smiled, clearly impressed. I had originally thought he was hitting on me, but to my delight he really meant to introduce me to this patron!

Hans George Berr, great grandson of the Archduke Esterase of Austria, was writing a book on Nepal and lived in the European section of Kathmandu.

Hans George was the most fascinating man I had ever met up to that point and through him, I eventually met all the top people in Nepal from the cousin of the King, to British and European businessmen, to the current tenth-generation silversmith for the King and finally the head Lama of Nepal, Tashi Gyaltsen, who was one of the teachers of the Dalai Lama himself.

It was here with Michel that I discovered this marvelous three-story house complete with all the European niceties and smack dab in the center of Kathmandu. Hans George had several people already living with him, including his manservant Stefan. Indeed he was looking for someone who knew how to paint the scenery and people of Nepal for the book he was writing.

When I first met him, he looked over my sketch pad with a businesslike attitude then offered me a job. He would put me up in a big room at his house. Also he would work out some exchanges for my paintings if he used them in his book.

Yes, Layla, being an artist opened every door on my travels and became my most valuable passport. I realized how very powerful it was to know how to draw, paint and photograph. An artist that can sketch or draw someone right in front of them, realistically, and capture something essential in that person, is someone revered in any country or in any language. I realized art has a way of transcending any time or place, and helped me make friends with a vast array of people.

I agreed to stay in Kathmandu in the house of my new Patron. It was my home base while in Nepal, somewhere to put my sitar. His house had a wall of all the music you could ever want from classical to rock and books on every subject. He admired artists, so I felt immediately welcome. I was impressed that, given he already had a few people staying with him, I had my own room with French doors overlooking terraced rice paddies leading up into the Himalaya foothills. It was beyond inspirational, it was blissful.

He hired me to paint several pictures. We briefly traveled to Pokhara, west of Kathmandu. There I captured the mountain overlooking the lake on canvas. Later I pictured people working in rice paddies and then different paintings of the outdoor markets, as well as other locations around Nepal. It was a great way to see the country, and George knew so much about the history since he was writing a book that he took pride in being my guide. I listened avidly.

But Hans George was a complicated man. He proudly handed me a photograph one day. I stared at it until he said, "that is my assistant, Stefan, and myself at a marvelous Christmas party at my castle!" He was proud of it and talked in his aristocratic Austrian accent, daring me to say something. The photo was a close up of himself and Stefan who was holding a huge plate of mushrooms. They were "magic mushrooms," full of psilocybin hallucinogenic content which can give anyone an instant high.

"All the best people were at my party, you know," he continued, "Anyone who was important and all major players in the Arts."

Hans George was about fifty; a bright-eyed, grey haired, rather thin man, who smiled with the kind of arrogance only the very rich can pull off. He looked down on me in more ways than one, but decided to share this picture with me, one of his secrets. Possibly to impress a pretty girl, or because he thought I would understand as an artist. *Artists don't have to take drugs to create great art, Layla, even if peer pressure makes it seem so. This plate of drugs was overkill.*

Just going to the party and meeting all the artists would have been enough for me, I thought to myself.

I tried not to act surprised, but just had to ask, "Your castle?"

"Yes, that was one of seven castles of mine in Austria, and it's the only one left. I gave the rest over to the state, with all the taxes and upkeep, you know," he said, regret edging his voice. "Now, let me show you something else...one of the prime exports of Nepal," he said.

His servant brought in a pipe and a pile of hash on a plate for him.

"It gets exported in diplomatic courier packs, and the King's nephew flies it out to Europe but keeps a little here for himself and for his friends."

I went pale and heard him say, "You look shocked, my dear. How do you think the drug trade worked? All the diplomatic pouches have such things. You know, every country has their secrets. Even yours. Don't be so naïve," he said with a patronizing tone in his voice.

That was the end of some of my illusions about politics, all right.

Chapter Twenty-Five

Painting Time

I DECIDED TO BURY MYSELF IN MY WORK. I TRIED OUT RICE PAPER WITH different colored inks and tested many techniques before I got the hang of it. Recreating the brilliant colors of the women's clothing as they bent over the rice paddies planting rows of green shoots was a ball! I had to experiment a lot to get it right and sometimes had ink running down the page, but final got it. I loved to work in oils and pastels—which are really the powdered form of the same minerals used in oil paints. That's why pastel paintings also last several hundred years.

When the time comes, I will show you all the art techniques I know, my dear Layla, and see what you like after experimenting for yourself! Creating can be the most fun.

It was almost an honor to work for Hans George, and I felt lucky to have the time to be able to use what I knew to illustrate this natural activity in a land so far away from my home in the West. He hired me to paint several other oil paintings, one a triptych (three panels of paintings that were attached with hinges) as well as paintings on rice paper.

I remembered when traveling to Pokhara, the prominent pointed-looking white-capped mountain in Nepal overlooking a lake, with Hans George who really wanted me to capture that area on canvas . It was almost a bust. *Oh, no! Just as I thought I couldn't make a mistake, here was an artist's nightmare.* I found to my chagrin that I ran out of purple paint! And a pure purple is a vital missing color when painting a mountain. *What to do?*

I decided to grind my own paint from the minerals in the rocks themselves and get the actual violet mineral pigment in quartz rocks where oil pigment comes from. Hans George knew where we could obtain this rock and I purchased some. Grinding it up took a lot of my time, but in the end it was worth it. Using some of my linseed oil with the powdered minerals, I was able to make the color purple. After that experience, the large painting I did of Pokhara with a Nepalese woman sitting down grinding out a meal in the foreground, was real to me and now I had the purple needed to set off the scene. The achievement was all the more satisfying because I did it myself. I learned to make my own paint and turned a problem around with a solution.

Wow! Independence felt great! I know you will also feel this way in your life, Layla, when you follow your own purpose.

Woman cooking

Chapter Twenty-Six

Silversmith and Son

T HE NEXT WEEK I HAD A VERY DIFFERENT EXPERIENCE THAT WAS MUCH more intimate and showed me a glimpse of what the Nepalese people were really like.

Entering the simple wooden dwelling, I looked past the dirt floor upon a touching scene between father and young son. The father, a silversmith whose family had created famous jewelry for Chinese dynasties going back many generations and now worked for the King of Nepal, was bent over the small fire holding a metal prong of some kind.

He was working on a necklace and his simple torch was turned down for soldering together a link of the delicate necklace. By the glow of that fire, I saw the young son bending forward so intent upon listening he ignored all else and wrapped his attention around his father. The father was telling him something in a low tone. He looked on his ten-year-old with such love and tenderness that I could both feel as well as see it from the bright glow of the fire reflected in his eyes.

It made me stop and pause at the door, silently taking in the scene before me. This was a special craftsman that was my good fortune to meet as well as visit with him in his shop when he was teaching his trade. I knew I was witnessing the rite of passage—a father passing his secrets on to his son, as it may have been going on for centuries before I stepped foot in his shop.

Hans George knew everyone of any fame in Nepal. I was there because he wanted to give me something, a present for all the paintings I was doing for him. He decided to have earrings made for me by the best in Nepal.

Hans George went on to say, "He makes jewelry for the King of Nepal, you know—the finest jewelry anywhere in the world. What kind of earrings would you like?"

I could hardly believe it. "Something that dangles and dazzles, but still light and not heavy on my ears," I told him.

He translated to the silversmith who first shook his head and then seemed to get an idea and he smiled. He spoke quickly to Hans George, who translated to me. "He is going to do something very special for you. He has been working on making very light earrings, spheres and shapes out of silver that are hollow inside, so they are very light. This is intricate work since the spheres are only one and one-half inches in diameter and smaller, but if anyone can do it, he can."

The earrings he wanted to make had hand-tooled designs on the outside, and the way he was making them they spun around 360 degrees. I smiled and mouthed a "thank you" at him.

Sure enough, I was presented five days later with the most beautiful hanging earrings in silver, with spheres and shapes that were hollow inside and so light- weight I never even noticed them on me. He was so proud that I was happy with them. The one-of-a-kind earrings would never be able to be duplicated back home. It was another part of Nepal I carried back with me.

Silver earrings from Nepal

Chapter Twenty-Seven

Finding Simon Again

W HEN WAS I GOING TO SEE SIMON? I KEPT THINKING TO MYSELF. Feeling the strong urge now to go up into the Himalayas, I knew I had to follow my instincts and had heard from friends of ours that they thought Simon was still up in the foothills.

Would I find Simon up here? I thought as I said good-bye to Hans George and rode the old bus from Kathmandu to the last place I had heard from Simon, thirty miles south at Biratnagar, Nepal. As I got off the bus with my backpack, I noticed the scenery had changed from lush rice paddies in the valley to the rising foothills of wild grasses, few flowers, and scrubby trees. This is where trekkers embark for the foothills of the Himalayas and many of the upper villages can only be reached by foot. There were porters available as well as Sherpas for those going all the way up to Mt. Everest Base Camp. But I was only interested in reaching Simon, and anxiously looked around. *Where was he?*

"Do you know where the British Health post is?" I asked a knowledgeable looking man who I heard speaking some English. He pointed to a structure at the end of one of the main streets. It looked like it was large enough to house a few shelves of goods and there were both Nepalese and Europeans hanging around. I walked down towards the building and stopped inside the door, asking the American there, "Have you see an Englishman named Simon?.

"Of course," she replied, "Simon was just here. He's staying in that lodge up the road, right there," she pointed with a careless gesture. *I guess pointing is popular in Nepal and transcends language.*

As I walked over to the lodge, I was feeling self-conscious. *What if he doesn't want to see me?* I suddenly thought. But I trudged ahead, wearing my sturdy earth shoes, long Indian skirt and shirt and carrying my back pack. I ran my fingers through my long hair, licked my lips, and smoothed out my skirt while walking into the small entranceway. I was clean, but a little dusty from the bus ride, my pulse was racing with excitement. This was it, I would finally see him again after all my travels!

He was just inside and turned around staring at me. "Lynda!" he said with complete surprise and shock. "Where did you come from?"

"I just happened to drop in!" I said laughing, and then, "Really, I got here by bus from Kathmandu just now," I smiled. He looked a bit disheveled, but basically the same. I completely caught him by surprise.

"G'blime," he swore, "It is you!" he said starting to smile. Then he came over and gave me a big hug and kiss in a sudden gesture of welcome.

Something had changed, though, and I could feel it. "How long are you here for?" I asked him.

He looked concerned and a bit flustered. "I've been here for weeks now. I was just going to return to Kathmandu tomorrow, to catch my flight home," he said and then hurriedly added, "But we have all today and tonight."

I was trying to hide my disappointment, "Okay, I guess we can have some time together before you leave."

"How do you like Nepal? Have you been up to see Terry and Mary in the foothills yet?" he quickly asked me, trying to change the subject.

"No, that's where I'm headed next, trekking up to see them," I answered a bit too quietly.

"Well, they're working with the villagers and are the only doctor and nurse for many miles around, so they're very busy." He seemed to want to discourage me from going, but I was not easily dissuaded. I had come this far and I wasn't going to stop now.

"I have my backpack and will be trekking in the hills for the next month. I even talked to the Nepal Medical Trust about taking photos and paintings along the way, and they want to use them even hinted they need a photographer. So I may have a job in Nepal when I get back down from the foothills!" I told him proudly. He looked a little stunned.

"I'll be fine," I said, in case he cared. He still looked a little surprised again, like I might not survive or something and I laughed. "Don't worry about me, you're going home."

He became solicitous and asked me to have tea with him. It was a ritual for him that I had observed back in London where he asked for precise amounts of milk and sugar in his tea. When we sat down at the low table, it was Tibetan tea that was served— strong with butter in it from the water buffalo. The butter tasted like cream and added flavor. Of course Simon added sugar as well. As I sipped the tea I started to relax.

Simon was always used to being in control and this situation caught him off guard. We talked about Nepal as equals, sharing our experiences. He mentioned the people and their lifestyle, and I talked about my trip starting from Europe, leaving out some of the more passionate times with the men I met. I told him about entering Kathmandu Valley on a bus. He was curious, I could tell, and wanted to ask me why I came here. I was shy about letting him know it was because of him and talked more about the adventures I had.

He admired my determination and how I made it here. After a while he asked me if I wanted to stay overnight with him. I could tell that being together again brought out old memories of being lovers and our own travels together.

"I don't have a place yet," I said tentatively and he responded quickly.

"Stay with me here."

We went back to his room—a small space with a plain, low bed with mattress and Tibetan blanket, a table and chair with a lamp sending shadows up the walls in between its rays of light.

We smoked a little hash. It interested me about the connection that drugs had to romance and sex, if any, especially with Simon. I began to enjoy myself and relax, and so did Simon. Maybe the hash helped, but I wondered if I really needed it now.

I have to say it didn't have the same appeal for me anymore, Layla, and you'll probably have more romance and fun without the drugs!

We talked about travels and our observations of people and places. My view was more enthusiastic and spiritual, and I talked about my paintings and photographs while Simon went on about the people and how simple yet peaceful their lives were without all the modern conveniences. Thatch or mud and stone houses here were without refrigerators, stoves, furnaces, dishwashers, and no running water or bathrooms (*which is one thing we both agree was sorely missing*). Yet the people were bright, gentle, loving and fun without these "modern things."

We were deep in conversation, and I had as much to say as he did, which was a change. Usually I followed his lead. The rapport we had was a strong bond. He seemed to notice my independence and then said, "Time for me to go to bed. It's over here and there should be enough room," (meaning room for me) as he motioned to his bed. As I lay down next to him, we kissed and it was sweet, but short. He was going back to Toronto the next day to join his girlfriend, an airline stewardess, and seemed to be wrestling with being faithful. His eyes were on me, I could feel his heart pounding fast when he kissed me and felt the familiar pull. We still loved each other, but it was different now.

I realized I liked leading my own life independently going with what I really felt was right. My perceptions of life were an artist's, and I was basically a happy person inside when free to express that. Always searching and curious, I needed to find out what was real to me, not just told to me or something I read in a book. And now, even if I felt that tug of war with my feelings toward Simon, I didn't have to do something because of it. That realization hit me hard. I murmured sleepily to Simon I wanted to sleep now, snuggled up to him and closed my eyes. I don't know how long it took for him to get to sleep. Even if he was frisky and felt that sexual pull, I felt stronger resisting it and knew I could finally just be there with him, close friends and past lovers, without the sex.

I can be on my own now, happy again, was my last thought before I fell asleep in Simon's arms. I didn't know if I would ever see him again.

Chapter Twenty-Eight

Nigel and the Sherpa

THE NEXT MORNING SIMON LEFT ON THE BUS BACK TO KATHMANDU airport. He looked like he didn't want to go and even said, "I might be back sooner than you think." I found that curious.

But something tugged inside of me and I felt I had to continue my search, on my own, so over I went to the Nepal Medical Trust run by the English to inquire about anyone going up towards Mount Everest.

"Do you have anyone going up into the hills, trekking?" I asked. "I'm a painter and photographer and would like to join a group or a guide going up to the villages in the foothills. Some friends are up there, interning as doctor and nurse, and I want to visit them and also take photographs. I can't accept your offer of a job, but I will get you some great shots while trekking in the hills!"

The older Englishman there told me, "As a matter of fact my young health care volunteer, Nigel, is going up to deliver medicine to the health posts and he has a Sherpa guide. Maybe you could join them."

Elated with this news, I went straight over to where Nigel was staying and found him without much trouble because there weren't many tourists this far from Kathmandu except trekkers or mountain climbers. This was also the first leg of the trek up to the Mt. Everest Base Camp. After a little persuasion and letting him see my camera and art supplies, he agreed to let me join them.

"But you have to keep up, and contribute your fair share to the food," he said with typical British aplomb. Nigel was a tall, thin Englishman, and the young son of the rich British Protectorate of Hong Kong, I later found out. He loved hiking, had joined the British equivalent of the Peace Corps, and was somewhat at odds with his father from the gossip I heard. But I liked him right away, independent and ready to take a chance instead of the status quo. I was packed and ready to leave the next morning with Nigel and the Sherpa.

I looked forward to what was going to happen next up in the foothills of the mighty Himalayas.

Himalaya clouds in the foothills

Chapter Twenty-Nine

Touching Heaven

A FTER SEVERAL HOURS OF TREKKING, I STARTED TO ENTER ANOTHER space, another time and what looked like another world. I'm not sure why, but it was the first time I've had so much quiet and in such an enormous space.

Maybe you can understand or feel it too if you go up into the mountains yourself, Layla. There is a timeless quality many notice with awe.

Looking at the Himalayas rising above me at an impossible height it seemed like they touched the land of God above, the heavens, and the Milky Way in all their glory. At twilight they're especially omnipotent as the last rays of sun filtered over the rocks and snow, reflecting rainbow colors of light mixed with deepening shadows. The mighty mountains seemed blessed with a beauty that no human hand created. It made it all the more mysterious and beckoning while we were trekking through the hills.

I kept seeing changing shapes in the clouds, shapes that thrilled and inspired me. With the Himalayas, I imagined the overlapping peaks forming the outline of a beautiful woman. Hiking in her foothills I gazed on as she changed her mind and was instantly out-doing herself with the beauty of spring or creating static excitement in the air from a storm about to burst around the next bend—a constantly changing landscape, depending upon her mood—*kind of like my own.*

Mankind can't help but always admire this mountain cathedral reaching up to touch heaven with such brilliant stars rarely seen, sparkling brighter than mere diamonds.

I wonder if the mountain climbers who strive to mount her do so out of reverence and love, or just because she is there. I feel her flirtatious, mocking challenge to the male ego, calling out, *"Mount me! Make love to me if you can. But you will never have my soul. My spirit will always remain here."*

I have hiked all over the Rockies, throughout the States and the magnificent mountains in Canada at Banff. I saw the Alps, visited the mountains of Hawaii, but nothing, absolutely nothing, prepared me for the Himalayas. Constantly evolving, I witnessed the way the atmosphere as well as the landscape with all the vegetation changed so quickly here.

The mountains seem to say, "Long after your bones are dust, and the bones of all your children's children are dust, I will remain. *Immortal.*"

Backpacking medicine to the Foothills

Chapter Thirty

Trekking in the Foothills

I FIRST SAW THE NEPALESE CHILDREN COME THROUGH THE GRASSES AS the stalks parted in their wake. They looked from seven to eleven-years old, two boys and a girl, with the Nepalese light coffee skin and shining almond eyes. They were smiling while they shouted greetings. Dressed in cotton shorts or a shift, they came barefoot scampering through the high grasses to check us out when they saw us come over the hill.

Feeling like the pied piper when we entered village I was surrounded by chatter and laughter. Speaking Nepalese one of them touched my skirt, an Indian weave that went down to the top of my earth shoe sandals.

"They have never seen a white woman before," Nigel told me. "They are asking about you, where you are from, who you are," he further translated for me. "I am from America, and my name is Lynda," I told them.

Nigel translated. Their version of my name was something like "inda." As we kept walking, they cried out running around us, all excited. I quickly took out my Pentax Spotmatic camera to capture their images as they waded through the tall grasses. The plants and flowers had recently been soaked with the monsoon rains and the children's joy at being able to play outside in the sunshine again was infectious! I laughed with them as they pointed to me and my camera.

"Foto, foto," the children chanted while they walked into my picture, happy to be admired and uninhibited.

The people of Nepal seemed almost childlike and innocent to me because of the spontaneous, unselfconscious display of emotion in such a natural setting. It is an endearing quality I came to find in rural communities and children all over the world. Children always know if a person truly likes them. They gravitate to affinity and they just knew I loved kids. No translation necessary.

You have always been so aware of people, Layla. Since you were a few months old you selected only those you wanted to talk to. Your communication got through.

Trekking to the next village in the foothills meant getting an early start. We had to make it. We had to get to the next village before dark or we would be stranded out there, without food or lodging. It had been a good ten hour trek so far. Off I went with Nigel and the Sherpa porter, racing ahead of me even though he was carrying a large basket full of supplies weighing over fifty pounds on his back. My leather sandals and Indian skirt were holding up well and I dressed for comfort, if not for speed. Then the porter looked over at me, gave a smile, and challenged me to a race down the mountain trail. He nodded to the trail ahead and gestured for Nigel and I to try following. Nigel also had a large pack on his back since he was delivering health medicine to the outposts. I only had my own backpack and much less weight to hold me back.

The next thing I knew I was flying down the mountain trail and got to the point where my feet just knew where to step and what to do. I never faltered, but ran down the slopes of the hills chasing the Sherpa laughing as we went. At one point in time I actually had the feeling of flying over the trails, the foot-worn stones and packed earth from thousands of bare feet held no danger. I was flying high, exhilarated and pumping out those endorphins higher than any drug could provide

We made it!" This was the most grueling part of the trip and we did it. The health post owner and village head was gracious and generous. Each village we trekked to gave us food and shelter in exchange for Nigel's supplies and a few rupees. This trip for a month or two in the foothills would have never happened without the help of the porter, a Sherpa, and Nigel as well as the amazing villagers I met along the way. My exchange with the villagers was a painting, a portrait I did of them, or a photo and many hung them up on their walls with pride. I was so glad I could give them something back for all the priceless things they gave me.

When we reached a village, after eight to ten hours trekking, the first thing we did was to get introduced to the village head or "Elder" of that area. The head of the village was usually the one who owned and ran the makeshift trading post. Each of them was most gracious to us, since Nigel was delivering health supplies, vaccines and medicines they normally couldn't get. The owners usually fed us and put us up for the night in a spare room.

Exhausted, with tears running down my face, I plunked down in the room with my pack. We had just caught the last of the monsoon rains which always brought out the leaches. It rained just enough to make the trail muddy and I slipped and fell down into the rice paddies right on my butt, fortunately, since it was the most padded part of my body. But Nigel looked over at me, without a word he came over and had me sit down on the bench when we stopped in the village. He took off my pack and then looked down at my sandals. I looked down in shock. They were red.

There was blood running down my feet and onto my sandals. He lifted my long skirt and there were the leaches. I saw about five leaches on each of my feet, and to my horror they were wiggling a bit. Nigel looked at me and said he would take care of them. He gently pulled each of the attached leaches from my feet and put them in some kind of bowl for later disposal.

At that point I was numb and didn't feel much when he pulled them off. *At least I didn't feel them when we were trekking.* They were disgusting to look at, dark and filled with my blood. *How long had I been trekking with those hitchhikers sucking on me?* I wondered. Well, at least they only came out during the rainy season, and today was the last day of the monsoon. Relief flooded me, and as I go. my balance back again I thought of my family. *My brothers would have loved these critters for fishing in Minnesota, since they had no back off from baiting a hook with leaches.* I made a promise after this I would never touch a leach again, no matter how much my brothers teased me.

Another thing I noticed after visiting quite a number of villages was a discovery about the people of Nepal. They could be so generous despite poverty and they made great meals for us. There is so much space and beauty surrounding them, and they seemed to have a more relaxed attitude toward life. Families living in the same way for generations, doing things themselves, not dependent upon the mall or supermarket, raising and making their own food, weaving clothes, making pottery, creating brass bowls for serving, and designing jewelry of coral and turquoise, gold or silver, brass or copper. So many colors, so many types of goods, all spread out on a blanket, available in the open markets of each village we visited from Kathmandu to the upper Himalayas.

As I looked around the next village, I spotted men smoking cigarettes and pipes, sitting cross-legged haggling about prices, and women working on colorful dresses supplying the tea or maybe something stronger. They have a local beer and liquor that tastes a little like ouzo. Tibetan tea has butter in it, but you have to really taste the water buffalo butter to understand how creamy it is, just like milk. The yogurt, also made out of the rich water buffalo milk, is so creamy it's like a pudding. It was so tasty, I pretty much lived on it every day and found out later it was extraordinarily healthy for you with all the enzymes. That and the spiced vegetables with freshly killed and cooked chicken. Yum! It was so delicious, and makes my mouth water just thinking about it.

Food is an art as well as a science. And, also survival!

Open market day in the Himalayas

Chapter Thirty-One

Art of the Foothills

S OME OF THE VILLAGE ELDERS, LIKE BHARENDRA, ASKED ME TO EITHER photograph them or paint their picture, which was the same word to them, "Foto." It is what they also called "realistic paintings." I had brought my pastels, paints, and charcoal with drawing tablet and set to work on capturing their likeness. They invariably hung the picture up on the wall in a place of honor, with or without a frame. I was proud that I could use my talent to make them so happy.

To this day, somewhere up in the Nepal foothills paintings of mine may still be decorating the trading posts or houses. *Who knows?* They adored the realistic style I was trained in, and were fascinated watching me paint or draw their image.

For those who were very superstitious, a photo image or realistic painting could capture a person's soul. To the Nepalese my paintings were so different than they were used to, not like the Mandela of the Buddhists and Hindu designs so intricately done. I went into the open market in the village to see what they made.

How a painter, who knows about and studies color, light, dark, shadow, sunlight, and movement, sees the world is not how your ordinary person sees it, I realized later on. Every nuance in the shades of color, where the light hits especially, and the whole landscape of each environment is different. I saw that difference with my own eyes while traveling. For instance, take the shades of water—the intense blue of the Mediterranean in Italy and Greece, the light aqua of the Caribbean and Hawaii, the clear mountain springs, and the deep dark blue of the cold Pacific distinguishes each body of water and affects the landscape.

This tiny country was unusual. The jungles of Nepal's valley with hot yellows and warm greens, the mountains by Mount Everest base camp with cool blues and violets, vary dramatically within one small country. Each place is uniquely a world in itself, the light is different making the colors, the way it spills out upon the land with the time of day and location, illuminating or shading the buildings, landscape, or people.

The contrasts between America and Nepal are dramatic, Layla, and by reading this you will see what I mean. Actually Nepal and India were my view of the Orient, and they were so alien from where I came from. But in spite of that, I felt more back to nature—simple living outdoors, simple houses, simple lives and simple generosity. As the philosophers say, the simple things are the most profound.

Chapter Thirty-Two

The Tibetans of the Foothills

IN NEPAL THERE IS AN AIR OF MYSTERY AND MAGIC, WITH MONKEYS roaming the temples and exotic smells on the breeze in open air village markets high up in the foothills. Bright wool blankets, hand woven, were spread out on the ground. Displayed on the blankets were hand-made copper pots, clay pottery, and colorful cloth someone wove themselves along with a bounty of every type of edible vegetable and fruit. Most of these were new to me. But it was a typical shopping day for the Tibetans.

The clothing of Tibetans stands out in a group like a dark shadow mixed in among the faded Indian saris and Nepalese cotton pants, shorts and vests. But the long, thick, black, fold-over cotton jumper was the warmest protection against high mountain breezes. Seeing them come into focus, I noticed their thick Tibetan tunics reached their knees, tied on the side, with colorful blouses I could just make out underneath. Any color was set off nicely by the black-as-night tunics.

The villages were the main places you can see Tibetan women, who are tremendously shy. I barely heard them come over the hill, all eight of them at once, walking toward the outdoor market so soundlessly. I felt them before I saw them, their presence was so strong. They entered tentatively, and it was like they didn't want to venture far into unknown territory. Maybe too many people they didn't know. They talked to each other in low voices as their single braids hung down their back and swung back and forth as they walked. You could see their black hair shining and liquid almond eyes peeking behind thick lashes.

They wore amazing jewelry. I noticed they wore many pieces —coral, emerald, jade, silver, and gold. They looked over at me staring at them and held their heads up a little higher. *Guess I would too, if I was wearing gold and precious gems all over my body!* Later I learned that the Tibetan women wore the wealth of their family as a sign of their position and pride. From all the simple and dull colored cotton shorts and shifts of the Nepalese, the Tibetan women stood out like living, breathing holy temples lavished with gifts from their parishioners.

Since all the items for sale were spread out on huge colorful blankets, they had to navigate through beaten-copper bowls and bolts of silk and cotton material which added to the exotic colors. The scent of garam masala filled the air. The smells wafted over the market along with the sounds of animals braying and people talking. Some of Tibetans also manned their own blanket of wares. They were taller than the Nepalese and always seemed to talk in whispers among themselves. I heard them and wondered what they thought of me, the only white woman among the crowd. *What would they tell each other? Were they like all women, talking to female friends about their men or children? Asking advice or giving it? Or maybe talking about their hopes and dreams?* I'd like to think we had a bond there as I snapped their photograph, despite their cutting side glances that told me they were wary of my camera. *What did they think of modern conveniences?* Maybe they felt we were insane or stupid, "people who needed machines" to do what they did by themselves, using nature and simple things around them. They crafted some fine jewelry, so they were not without the Arts. Theirs was a simple life based on survival and family. I envied them just then.

Nigel broke me out of my reverie, coming up to me and not saying much, except, "We need some fruit and vegetables for meals. See if you can barter for them and take some rupees with you." Over I went to haggle with the merchants.

Later that night after a few beers, Nigel starting talking more about his own travels. I found out a bit more about Nigel's father, the British Protectorate of Hong Kong—an imposing figure but not much of a dad. Nigel went his own way, shunning the money, and ended up in a non-profit organization delivering health medicine up in the hills of Nepal. He truly was like a cross between a rebellious hippie and a Peace Corps volunteer. Young, tall and thin, he had muscles of steel from the trekking. I liked him immediately and we became fast friends. What we had was mutual respect and reality because we both spoke English.

Well, he did and I guess he would say I spoke American.

One thing we did have in common was love of music, and I knew many of the British musicians, having grown up during the Beatles era. He surprised me with his knowledge and simplicity. How profound I found the magic of Nepal and the people was due in large part because of Nigel and what he showed me on that long trek up in the foothills.

Coming into the village preparing for market day high in the Himalayas

Chapter Thirty-Three

Music of the Mountains

M USIC WAS CREATED TO RELIEVE THE EFFECTS OF TIME ON IMMORTAL *beings*—the saying came to mind from a writer friend. Having already learned that Nepalese and Tibetans believe in past lives, that the spirit lives on, I wondered, *would their music reflect that?*

Exhausted from trekking for eight to ten hours a day in the hills for the last week or two, at first I thought I must be day dreaming or asleep on my feet. I heard a faint sound, and when I heard it again it sounded like tinkling and a rhythmic beat. I wondered if Nigel and the Sherpa heard it, too, or if it were only me. *There it was again!* Like bells dinging and a drum beating. Then, some kind of eerie flute was heard. The music was enchanting, mesmerizing and so fitting considering that I was in one of the most exotic places in the world. But where were the sounds coming from? I turned toward Nigel and he nodded at me and smiled. I wasn't crazy, he heard it, too.

We kept walking toward the sounds, which kept getting louder and louder, and as we rounded a corner I saw them. Three Sherpa porters were sitting cross-legged on a blanket on the ground, right near the trail on a flat slip of earth jutting out to the left with nothing but mountain below and all around them. The trail itself was made up of compact earth worn down by the mortal feet of many generations of what I thought of as the Greek god Mercury's assistants: the Sherpa and porters of the Himalaya foothills who delivered supplies and facilitated communication to all the villagers in this region. They were often the only link people had with the outside world.

I looked over and they were playing simple hand-made instruments—what to me looked like a type of flute, crude drums, and some kind of cymbals. I have no other words to describe them in my solely Western-educated language. They were that foreign to me. Yet music has common ground anywhere in the world. People instantly recognize it without words.

The sounds were eerie, yet delightfully lighthearted. We pitched our tent near the porters, who were spread out under the stars around a small campfire. I went to sleep hearing the music and dreaming of things of another time and space. To me the frequency of the sound waves themselves, the breaths, the cadence, the rhythm, and the way the instruments were handled could never be duplicated again so I basked in the sounds, memorizing it. The music seemed to burst forth telling the magic and mysteries of Nepal with each note. Leaving it up to my imagination as I lay there, I could see paintings in my mind's eye—the hues and images that represented the notes they played. I was painting a symphony in my mind.

My symphony would include the sounds of Monsoon rains falling, water buffalo drinking in the streams, the trees and bushes whispering when we passed growing sparser the higher we got, and sounds representing the stunning mountains of the mighty Himalayas, the white of snow reflecting and changing colors with the passing hours of daylight into night. It was just before the final black of night and I witnessed the glow of the last ray of light fading into a starry, starry sky so dense it looked unreal. I was there, part of it all. The line between looking and dreaming faded. I drifted off still hearing the music.

When the mood of the music changed, in my mind's eye I saw people with tanned skin, black shining hair, and almond shaped eyes smiling. They were simple people dressed in cotton shifts or shorts and vest, barefoot or sandaled like me. The scene then broke up into millions of people, holding up their hands as I floated by ethereal, flying slightly above them. They were reaching out to me as I took in their thoughts and blessings and gave hope back to them with my mind.

The dream reminded me I had a mission to accomplish, something I needed to do in life that would help people. *I was ready and really wanted to find out what that was, Layla, because at that point I had no idea!*

The next morning we left early, getting a jump on the next village. I had never worked so hard in any hiking experience as I did with the insistence of the porter and Nigel. The fact that every muscle in my body felt like it was working to the max didn't take away from the exhilaration of flying down the paths in the Himalaya foothills, as if my feet knew every step ahead of time.

I was so out of my head during the trekking that I kept remembering how it was when I was very young and saw myself on the ceiling, looking down at my own body. Being "out of my head" seemed natural.

Suddenly I was in my room at age three, looking down at my body lying in bed. I was on the ceiling in one corner, out of body, and my mom was there down below me. She was rubbing my back, soothing me so I would go to sleep. How many times did she come and rub my back when I couldn't sleep? She knew something was happening, but later on I discovered little kids are often out of their heads and flying. It's something I honestly looked forward to, and she accepted. But I'm always curious to find out what others think about it too.

We didn't have to talk. The porter and I just "knew" how each other felt, and how glorious it was to see the hills of Nepal fly by us with snow-capped mountains in the background. It was one of those sunny days after the monsoon rains, and we had trekked for a good eight hours. As I glanced up I could see the beginning of sunset touch the top of the mountains with a pale pink hue. I felt myself slow a bit as I wondered where the next village was. Usually we had reached one by now.

Almost like he read my thoughts, Nigel said, "We camp out tonight outside, with the Sherpas and porters, just around the next bend." He was taking out a small tent he had packed. As I raced ahead, I started to hear those strange sounds again. At first they were faint, little tinkling bells heard from a distance with that pounding beat in the background. And, then I saw it.

Spread out before me, was a bend in the cliff trail and rounding the cliff face through a spray of mist touching my face, I blinked at what I saw through the mist, for we were in the high foothills where we were actually walking through clouds. A group of Sherpas, dressed in only simple cotton shorts or pants and vest, barefoot and sitting cross-legged on the ground or on a blanket, were sitting there with some kind of homemade instruments by a fire. The music they were playing was haunting me again.

One had what appeared to be a Jew's harp fashioned out of metal. He was fingering and playing exotic soulful tunes. The use of sharps and flats again and the melodies they made were foreign to me and pure Nepal, but delightful still. One had a homemade drum that he was beating in a certain way and another had a kind of flute that produced melancholy sounds with repetition that reminded me of Arabian knights or horses galloping past sand dunes.

My imagination took off and for an hour I was transfixed again. When I came to, I realized I had sat down by the fire, still with my pack on my back and was the object of much interest, being the only female there. The Sherpa this high in the foothills had not seen many white Western women, if any at all. Mostly men come this way to go up to the Mount Everest Base Camp for mountain climbing, so I was a strange sight with shoulder-length red hair and green eyes. Maybe I scared them a little, since I was taller than they were, but they were definitely amused at my reaction. I loved the whole scene—their music, with all of them grouped around the fire. They could tell I was charmed.

When Nigel gave them some of our food supplies they made a whole meal for all of us. Later we went back to our tents with full bellies and happy hearts as the Sherpa unrolled straw mats to sleep around the fire.

With the utter quiet you only feel when in the presence of a great mountain range far from any city, I felt at peace. I know from being up in the Rockies in Canada and the States the silence can have a profound effect. Like music. I created a poem on the spot.

My Ode to the Himalayas

Glacier white, pristine
Untouched for centuries
Jagged profiles of sharp faces
Blending by gradients into a vast panorama
The wisps of wind-blown snow
Seen at a distance
Look like whirlwinds or tiny tornados on the sea of white
And the backdrop of a frozen tsunami of rock
The feeling of vastness all around
It doesn't make you feel small
But rather uplifts the spirit higher
The thrill of being there
The space, the time, the exotic people, the place
The charged atmosphere around me
And the thrill of feeling so alive!

Bridges in the mountains

Chapter Thirty-Four

The Gurkha Warrior

W E WERE ALMOST TO THE VILLAGE WHERE TERRY AND MARY WORKED. We had been trekking in the hills for weeks now. Each night we slept in a different village.

As we rounded a bend in the path through the hills after hours of trekking with little water left, we saw an old hut to the side of the path. Literally it looked like it would fall down any minute like some abandoned barn. The roof was made out of thatching and the structure had some kind of distressed wood with bamboo poles. The walls were mud or clay in deep brown, rust and ochre colors. It looked like it had been scorched by the sun for a very long time. The Sherpa signaled for us to drop our backpacks and rest. It was a sort of drinking spot, and when we entered I could see dusty stools and a small wooden bar with various bottles of alcohol and drinks on the top of an ancient wooden counter, scarred and scraped from the wear and tear of countless glasses from porters stopping for a quick drink. Nigel ordered water and tea with the traditional water buffalo butter and some sort of sweetener.

Sitting at the end of the bar was a weather-beaten older man, with copper-colored, wrinkled skin like tough leather. He was drinking what looked like a homemade brew. He was alone and glanced over when we came in. The Nepalese are short people, but this guy looked big because of how muscular and very fit for his age he looked, even if he was near sixty.

He looked as dried out as the hut, with a lot of grey in his hair, and he wore the usual Nepalese faded cotton shorts and vest jacket with the addition of a heavy belt. He seemed to me like he could take care of himself, as well as

117

anyone who might dare to cross him! I was fascinated by his wary, intelligent look, frowning as he eyed me. His staring was unnerving. But, I must have made a strange sight, a white woman so high up in the foothills! Eyeing my red hair and green eyes, he couldn't help but see I was not nearly as tan as the rest of our little group. Curiosity got the better of him when I took out my sketch pad, held it in front of me like a shield, and used my pencils and pastels to draw him. His next move would tell the story, *whether he was going to tear up my sketch or hit me!* I thought, from the intensity in his look that he must have seen way too much in his life time and I wanted to capture it on paper.

He made a move toward me, scraping his stool across the floor and plunking it down right next to me. I felt uneasy with his staring at my artwork. Turning to him, I saw he sat with eyes widened, and his eyebrows raised. Then he grunted and I flinched.

Nigel, who spoke Nepalese, quickly stepped over and struck up a conversation with him, explaining that I was an artist and asking if he would mind if I painted his picture. He drew back and looked surprised at how I had captured his likeness in a few short strokes and slowly nodded an okay. Then he scraped his stool back to where it had been and sort of posed for me. When I finished about a half hour later, I showed him the painting with trepidation. He was startled, staring at the likeness for the longest time, and then told Nigel something.

Translating, Nigel said, "He wants to buy the painting from you."

I told him, "What can he offer for it?" which Nigel relayed to the man. He took a long time telling Nigel something and then took out a wooded scabbard with a long curved sword inside and I cried out a bit in surprise. *Actually to me it looked like some kind of machete and I could imagine what he did with it!* It was very long, with a scabbard that had intricate carvings on it. I stared at it as Nigel told me the story.

The man told him that he was a Gurkha warrior, retired now, but one of a group made up of the fiercest fighting men in World War II working with the British. It looked like the sword scabbard had notches on it for the men he had killed! Each notch had a story to it. He was offering it to me for the painting and this was a great honor. He told Nigel the story of one of the battles he was in, and needless to say Nigel edited it down by the time he told me.

I accepted the sword in exchange for his portrait and took it with a bow to the Gurkha. I couldn't help feeling I was departing with a piece of history in my hands. I had to find out more about the Gurkha warriors and questioned Nigel as we trekked, "Nigel, what can you tell me about these fascinating Gurkhas?"

"Well," he began, "they are renowned for their fearlessness in battle during the Second World War. They were drafted from Nepal, after a skirmish with the British who saw their fierceness and were impressed. The British found a way to ally with them and fought alongside of them after that. Better to have a Gurkha on your side than against you!" he laughed.

"But the man we met must be very old," I said.

"Yes, that's a bit sad. So many Gurkhas from that time populate these hills and some do little except drink liquor and tea. But they are still revered for having brought about peace. The younger ones are still in service to the British."

"I know that Nepal is also a haven for Tibetans who were displaced when the Communists took over and did such cruel things in Tibet," I said frowning.

"Oh, that was a travesty. The Chinese Communists slaughtered thousands of peaceful monks when they invaded Tibet. Nepal is a buffer zone between the Communists and India, ruled by a King and royal family. They managed to create a peaceful country despite everything going on. The Gurkhas as a group are amazing and fierce. Maybe the Gurkhas had something to do with it," he said thoughtfully. "I heard one of the stories about them."

"Tell me, please," I begged. Nigel looked at me indulgently and began speaking.

"Apparently there was a Nepal war of 1812 where the British sent in thirty thousand troops against twelve thousand Gurkhas, arrogantly thinking they would take Nepal by storm. Just the opposite happened, and the Gurkhas fought the British to a standstill. There is a British monument inspired by that battle, with an inscription saying *they fought their conflict like men and in the intervals of actual conflict showed us liberal courtesy*. For the British, this is a high compliment! A short time later during another incident, British

Lt. Frederick Young leading a group of soldiers were surprised by a force of Gurkhas, masters at guerilla warfare. The soldiers, upon seeing the fierce Gurkhas unsheathing their swords, yielded and ran away, leaving the British officers to face the Gurkhas alone.

"The officers with Young leading them remained and held their ground even when completely surrounded. This greatly impressed the Gurkhas who asked them why they didn't run. Young said that he didn't come this far to run away, he came to stay. This made the Gurkhas think twice about us Brits, but he was still their prisoner. Luckily they didn't kill him. He ended up a captive of the Gurkhas for about a year and during that time the Gurkhas developed a deep respect for Young and the British fighting spirit, as we call it. Eventually, through the friendship developed with Young, and the promise of good pay and quarters as well as a good fight," said Nigel with a wink, "the Gurkhas decided to join the British. To this day they are still famous as the most fierce and absolutely fearless fighters England has ever seen."

I thought about the Gurkhas as we trekked on to the next village, and what stories they could have told from their perspective. It made me wish I could get inside their heads and know more about their culture and language.

Someday, I will go back.

As for the Gurkha sword, I decided to bring it home and present it to my father. I was curious what effect it would have. As we kept trekking in the hills, I thought a lot about the sword and knew that it would be another reminder of this wondrous place and the people far away I wanted to remember forever.

Gurhka Warrior sword

Chapter Thirty-Five

Whirling Dervishes

I*T WAS THE MUSIC THAT GOT MY ATTENTION AGAIN, LAYLA. YOU ALWAYS respond so well to music, so hopefully you can understand the effect it had on me.*

Arriving at the village of Terry and Mary up in the hills, I saw their make-shift hospital and living quarters. They greeted me warmly and offered all of us a meal and a place to sleep. I must have conked out immediately, we were so tired.

Now, as the sun was setting I remember hearing the sounds coming from a distance through groggy, sleepy ears and decided to go find out what was happening. A festival! They had the same home-made instruments I heard the porters play in the foothills, but many more of them and in unison.

I left Terry and Mary's small wooden house and went down to the village as the afternoon light went golden and weaving into dusk. I was not prepared for what I saw next.

The villagers were in a large circle surrounding three dancers swaying to the sounds coming from a group of Nepalese musicians. The beat changed and they started swirling around in circles to the music, faster and faster, their costumes whipping around them like a skirt of smoke. People were clapping and chanting along enthusiastically with the ever-increasing beat. The three men were wearing headgear that looked like horns on a kind of hat with strips of rags hanging down several feet around them as well as the rag skirts around their waist, swinging when they turned wildly in circles.

Terry leaned over and in a confidential tone told me, "They're the Lackeys, the Devils, or what you may call whirling dervishes, and represent the evils of the world.. The music hit a fever pitch and just at the crescendo a young boy stepped out, beautifully dressed in a red silk costume holding a long sword. He was young and handsome, looking like someone out of the Arabian Nights, and even wore the pointed shoes! He walked in a slow exaggerated way brandishing the sword over the Lackeys as the pounding of the beat rose up, pulsing past the breaking point. *What was he going to do with that big sword?*

Suddenly he lifted the sword high above his head and swiftly brought it down. I held my breath and closed my eyes for a second. *Oh, God, oh, God! What did I walk into?* When I opened them I saw he missed the Lackeys, who dropped down low in the crowd, spinning under the arms of the people in a circle around them, and disappeared out of sight.

In the mass confusion the Lackeys seemed to vanish. Triumphant, the boy raised his sword high again to the loud cheering of the crowd. "The boy represents Krishna, and his killing the Lackeys means another year the Devils are vanquished, so their world is safe again," whispered Terry in my ear.

At that point all the villagers started dancing and singing. Someone pulled me into a circle and I danced uninhibited with the crowd, and used some of my ballet training to do pirouettes or turns to the great amusement of the people. I was filled with joy and the people sensed I was in that same rapture they felt and welcomed me. It was a long time before I crawled in bed, exhausted, my own devils vanquished, too, for a time. I dreamt of Simon and wondered if I would see him again soon.

In the morning I was back at my sketchpad. I worked in oils and pastels and it was such a privilege to capture what I saw. I felt so lucky to be able to use what I knew to illustrate this natural activity in a land so far away from the West where I was born.

I was back in the swing of painting and had a million ideas! Now that I had seen Simon and trekked the hills, I was ready to get back to work and longed for home. After spending time with Terry and Mary, who were tending to the villagers, I bid them a fond goodbye and started on my journey back down to Kathmandu.

Whirling Dervishes

Chapter Thirty-Six

Coming Down from Heaven

WHEN I CAME DOWN FROM THE MOUNTAINS, I HAD TAKEN PHOTO-graphs all along the way of the people in remote villages. I stopped in to see the manager of the British Nepal Medical Trust in Biratnagar, and after seeing my photos and sketches he asked if I wanted a job here.

He gave me the option of staying in Nepal, working with the Trust doing the photographs and promotional materials they sorely needed. I would even be paid. Well, it was overwhelming at the time, and I took a while to think it over.

"We want to hire you because we need an artist's eye and someone able to see the aesthetic possibilities in Nepal to present to others. You captured the feeling of the Nepalese people and places you went, and can make it real to our potential visitors. It's a permanent position and you could stay in Nepal on a visa for as long as you wanted." I felt flattered and valued as an artist, but also felt a strong tug of homesickness.

"I'm sorry, it's a great offer and really tempting, but I have to go back home soon," I told him. It was so hard to turn down, but I missed my family and friends. I ended up selling him my photos for their use in promotion.

I wonder where I would be now, if I had taken him up on the offer? Official photographer to the Royal family of Nepal? Exotic art painter with a sought-after gallery of paintings high in the Himalayas? Writer and illustrator of travelogues in the Far East? Or a part-time tour guide for the English-speaking tourists and still hiking in the Nepalese hills sleeping on straw mats! But, alas,

I will never know. My choice was to go back home, and I really felt it was the right choice.

When I got back to Kathmandu, Simon had come back to Nepal again and we met briefly. I wondered why he flew back to Nepal after being away for only a few weeks, but he shrugged and merely said he missed it. *Why was he back? Did he miss me, too?* I had a feeling that he did miss me and sensed he felt protective and wanted to make sure I was safe.

He introduced me to his friend, Jay, a pre-med student from England, who was interning to be a doctor. When I probed Simon about why he came back, he explained, "I got back to Toronto and realized I missed the simple life in Nepal and had left too soon. I knew I needed more time here." I wondered if he still cared about me in a romantic way, but then decided it didn't matter. I was simply glad to see him again. Even though we had a great time in Kathmandu, he left for Toronto again a few days later, but his friend Jay stayed on.

Chapter Thirty-Seven

Dangerous Deception

JAY VISITED ME AT HANS GEORGE'S PLACE AND WAS FULL OF QUESTIONS.
"Are you still with Simon?" he asked me. I let him know we had broken
up, but I was still open to the possibility of getting back together at some
point. "Ok, but right now you're not his girlfriend, am I right?" he persisted.

"Yes, that's right," I reluctantly told him.

"Well, how about showing me around? There are places in Kathmandu I
haven't seen, and I'd like your company," he said with a smile.

About then the rickshaw with a Nepalese man riding a surrey-topped
bicycle rickshaw, pulled up next to us and we jumped in. We were soon
having fun traveling all around the city, tasting different types of food with
all the Indian and Nepalese spices in delicious sauces. I had never tasted
some of the spices or sauces before and liked them so much I bought some
spices to take back home with me. Jay laughed and told me stories of England
and getting through medical school. We had a good time until nightfall.

He took me to his youth hostel telling me, "You've got to see this, something I want you to try." I was wary, but he was Simon's friend so I trusted
him. *I should have listened to my instincts.*

What he wanted to show me, as he reached into his suitcase and drew out
a package in brown paper wrapping, was a ball of something brown. "It's
some of the best hash in the country," he said as he unwrapped it.

Simon and I had smoked some good hash a few times, made of super
concentrated marijuana. As far as I knew, it wasn't "hard stuff" and not
addictive, so I told him, "Sure, I'll try some." I didn't really need it, but didn't

want to appear a spoilsport with Simon's friend and was game for some fun. He took out something that looked like oily light-brown dough and said I should ingest it for best results, like a hash cookie.

As Jay gave me a small doughy ball of the brownish substance, his exact words were, "Swallow it down, doctor's orders.. He also gave me a bottle of Nepalese beer to wash it down. After about twenty minutes, he sidled up to me very assertively. I started feeling sick to my stomach and asked him, "What did you give me?.

He said he thought it would relax me, "It can help with inhibitions," and gave me the come-on look that said more than words. I was suddenly afraid and felt more pain in my stomach. I somehow pushed my way out of his place and knew I had to get out and go back to Hans George's house.

I barely got to a rickshaw, shoved some rupees in the driver's hand saying "Go, go" and mumbled Hans George's address.

I heard Jay, behind me, shouting from the door, "Hey, what's your hurry? Come back!" Everything faded and went black after that.

The next thing I knew, I was opening my eyes and saw Hans George, his assistant, Stefan, and Harka, the Nepalese house boy, all staring down at me. They had me on a mattress on the floor, hovering over me, all looking very pale (*which was especially telling, since Harka's skin was usually dark!*)

"You scared us to death! We almost lost you. Do you realize you almost took pure opium! We had to have your stomach pumped," Hans George said anxiously, looking at me. I was so confused and out of it I didn't know the full story until the next day.

Apparently, I had eaten a small part of an ounce of opium—you know, the raw sticky stuff that contains morphine which can be made into heroin. It was almost enough to kill me, but I guess I was too stubborn to die. All I could think of was what a wonderful colorful dream I had had. But in waking up I felt like my whole aching body was screaming. My stomach rolled over in pangs of pain like I just fell out of a clothes dryer, the old kind that spin around off balance.

I was still sweating a lot and Harka showed me how many wet towels he had gone through nursing me. During the last twenty-four hours Hans George had been so anxious he almost called the American Embassy to get my family here. Maybe he thought I needed the last rites. *Yikes!* He looked so relieved when I woke up. I was touched. "Silly girl, don't ever scare me like that!" he said in his Austrian accent.

I later learned that Jay had left Nepal for England, and that through his connections as a pre-med student he prescribed drugs for himself and others. He had access to every type of drug and was selling some of it to get through school. *The med school drug pusher*, I thought to myself in disgust and felt embarrassed that I had fallen for it. Much later I learned of Jay's death by overdose. It was a sad ending and such a waste of life.

Peer pressure to take drugs never has a happy ending, Layla, and I hope you'll handle it better than I did.

After that I swore off all hard drugs, even if they were prescribed by a doctor. I remembered my mom telling me of my grandfather, a doctor from Sweden, who made tinctures of natural ingredients, plants that were medicinal, and was great at listening to his patients which sometimes was as effective as anything else. He had a large following in Minnesota and that was when I saw the great value of more natural methods. *Works for me!*

I had to go through hell and back to learn my lesson about drugs. Almost over-dosing was the push I needed in my search for the answers to questions about my life, and I hoped and wondered if at the end of my search I would find the truth. *What was the best way out of the traps of this world? How do I gain real enlightened awareness of the spiritual side of who I am and also what I can really do?* Drugs sure were not the answer. What was the answer?

The impact of that time was etched in my mind. Sometimes people become addicted to prescription drugs, too. From then on I handled all health matters with natural remedies, and never went to hospitals. My view was that hospitals and nursing homes were where people got sick, and died, whether by doctor error, the wrong drugs, infection from others or complications.

Many years afterwards, I look back at the time I made that choice to be careful about using drugs and to use natural methods and vitamins or natural foods instead. It really stuck. The only thing I fear is the dentist. *Oh Yes, the sound of the drill gives me chills, even to think of!* But I hear they have soundless laser treatments now, so even there I have hope.

I was still looking at the spiritual side of life and needed more answers.

Chapter Thirty-Eight

Tashi Gyaltsen, Lama

A S I HAVE MENTIONED BEFORE, I WAS TRYING TO FIGURE OUT WHAT IT was that happened when I was a small girl, from about age two to five, at night when I viewed my body from a distance and felt so free.

I know it used to worry my mom, and she would rub my back and softly talk me down until I went to sleep, but she didn't know what it was either. I was so young it was hard to communicate what was happening to me, but I saw my body lying in bed—looking at it from up in the corner of the ceiling where I hung out. *What was that about, anyway?* I told her I was floating, that I was up above her and felt high up in the air and that it felt a little funny, but good. She was concerned but not afraid, and knew I had trouble getting to sleep. No one told me what that experience was, until I met the Lama.

I think children everywhere will know what I mean, Layla, and you may already know. The trick is how to express something as a child that you don't quite understand yourself. I really wanted to find out and was frustrated at not being able to explain it.

Through Hans George Berr I was introduced to His Holiness, the Lama, Tashi Gyaltsen, who was the spiritual head of all Buddhists in Nepal. I hoped he may finally answer a few questions for me about these out-of-body experiences.

I guess George was a bit worried about me and wanted to point me in the right spiritual direction! He set up a time for me to go to the main Buddhist temple and meet the Lama who was revered as a teacher, and his young assistant, Thubten, who was educated in the West and knew English well and translated for the Lama. Thubten let me know the Lama had heard from Hans George that I was a painter. Hans George knew everyone in Nepal, so I wasn't surprised. I suspected George had told him about my overdose and asked the Lama if he could help me, spiritually.

Thubten was fascinated by my paintings. I also found out quickly that Thubten, the young monk, still had an amorous side to him. After talking to him at length about a monk's life and being the Lama's assistant, we established a connection. Then impulsively he said he wanted to show me something. I was curious and asked what it was. He briefly showed me his large erection, which was hidden underneath his robes. When I gasped and quickly shifted my gaze to his face, I saw that his expression was proud and playful at the same time—very innocent, somehow.

I guess he thought it would prove he was still a man, or maybe he thought it was some kind of compliment or maybe his time in the West polluted his values, or maybe, just maybe, he was lonely and wanted to let me know that monks could still have sex. I think he was trying to shock me. In any case, I wasn't really shocked as much as surprised at what he did! Looking back, I can't help but smile at his cheekiness.

Thubten was the one who translated for the Lama and met everyone, including all the Westerners. After he'd looked through my sketchbook, he immediately became serious and escorted me into the large temple room. He told me I should sit across from His Holiness, the Lama, and paint. My stomach felt fluttery and I found myself holding my breath but told myself to calm down and take a deep breath, and go forward into this newest adventure. *I grabbed my pencils and pastels and dove right in.*

Chapter Thirty-Nine

Lama's Prediction

A T FIRST I THOUGHT THE LAMA MUST LIVE IN THE LARGE COLORFUL Stupa—the Buddhist temple that looks like a pyramid with a large round dome on top and steps going up with a Buddha face painted on the dome and lots of saffron, cinnamon, and yellow ochre pennants flying in the breeze. But no, that was used in ceremonies. I was going to Headquarters.

It was an ancient looking temple, at least several hundred years-old, with a huge room in the center where the Lama took audience. Smaller rooms opened off the main central room and I wondered what was in there. To my amazement I later found out there were monks in each room praying.

When Thubten ushered me into the room I saw a small figure seated on a rug thrown on the bare floor inside the temple. His Holiness radiated a calm, powerful presence from where he sat in the bare setting. Thubten indicated that I should sit on cushions about twenty-five feet across from the Lama. That's when I learned that Tashi Gyaltzen had been one of the teachers of the famous Dalai Lama, and was now the revered spiritual head of all Buddhists in Nepal. Even though he was small and grey haired, there was an immense presence about him I could actually feel.

The first thing that struck me when I met him was how he looked at me. One of his eyes seemed to look far off into the distance to the side and the other one looked straight at and through me. I took out my paints, and with pad in hand I started to capture that discrepancy in his eyes, the best I could. Spending a lot of time sitting across from the Lama, who was cross legged and never moved much, I studied him carefully.

Surrounding us, I began to notice the Nepalese and Tibetan people being quietly escorted over to kneel down next to him, one at a time. The Lama would murmur things, the Nepalese would talk with a questioning look on each individual's face, the Lama would respond, and the person would look like he realized something, thank the Lama and quietly leave in the direction from which he or she came. This was happening all afternoon. I was so curious I had to ask.

"What's going on?" I asked Thubten, who then patiently explained to me the procedure.

Villagers would come to ask the Lama about some serious problem they had and the Lama would tell them a kind of parable, example or story with a message, to make them think. They would get the idea or message from what was said and leave. The Lama made a point to let them solve their own problems, and they were expected to go back and handle their situations using the insights they had gained from the Lama's story. He was in a true sense giving audience to those seeking his guidance and directing them to think for themselves.

"Wow, I like that!" I told him. "It was exactly what intelligent and wise people I knew back in the West told me. This is so cool! It's like a light went on inside me," I told him further. A friend had told me "don't solve another's problem, just give guidance and let the person solve it." The Lama seemed to be a true believer in showing the way but letting the person work things out themselves. Later on I was to remember this principle and would realize this idea could revolutionize education. It made people think for themselves and figure out how to deal with things, rather than dictate, make them memorize stuff they would probably never use, or spoon feed a solution. I realized it was the creative way, and felt it really did increase a person's self-worth and self-confidence.

I felt touched and privileged to be able to present my painting to the Lama later that afternoon. When he saw it, his eyes sparkled with delight and he chattered in merriment, in the sing-song language of the Tibetans. Thubten told me he said that I "got his eyes right." He then indicated he wanted me to stay the night in the spare guest room, which was a great honor reserved for only a few. He was going to chant for me that very night.

But first I was to sit down on cushions across from the Lama with a low table set between us, and was served the traditional Tibetan meal of rice and beans, bowls with vegetables and a little meat in spicy sauces. I used my hands to eat, as was the custom, but always after washing my right hand thoroughly. The meal was flavorful and fresh, and may have tasted better than it was because I was suddenly so famished. But it was nourishing and had a nice bite to it. After washing my hands at the end, as well as my face, I was escorted to my room to retire.

What I found was a "spare" room in both senses of the word, for this one had only a pallet and mattress for a bed. The room was devoid of anything else, with bare stucco walls framed in wood. A dirt floor was covered in a rug that was of thick wool with Tibetan design. I could make out a Mandela pattern in fading colors of red wine, dark green and golden yellow. It had one window open to the outside. I was tired, so I lay down to sleep and immediately fell into a deep slumber.

My dreams were in Technicolor—a long series of moving pictures of various people in different situations. I recalled seeing Simon as we were in Toronto, Canada, and what he said to me then was vivid and clear, yet troubling. This dream was full of worry, anxiety and uncertainty.

Next the dream shifted to the images of my travels across Europe to Nepal; scenes and people I met as I traveled. Just as quickly it changed to different times and different places I didn't quite recognize and yet they felt familiar. It felt like times long, long ago. The faces I saw filled me with longing and some with dread. But all along, in these dreams, I definitely had the feeling I was moving, floating slightly off the ground and a bit out of my body.

All of a sudden the dream scenery shifted dramatically and I saw thousands of people spread out over a tropical land. They had their hands raised up, talking cheerfully, almost cheering. I was slightly above them just skimming along over their heads. There were endless hands, thousands of all nationalities, reaching up from all directions, and I seemed to float above them and touch each person's hands as I went by, slowly traversing the land. There was a look of hope in their eyes that stood out and with all my being I was pouring out love, friendship and felt myself opening up to them, intending them well, and seeing them smile back in recognition. It was a powerful feeling that this might have something to do with my future and that I was supposed to help people.

I was asleep, I swear it. But something was bothering me—some faint tinkling sounds interrupting my thoughts woke me. It was pitch black in the room and I knew it was the middle of the night, but I got up anyway. Sliding out of the door to the back garden area, I could feel a pull from the stars, like they were calling out to me.

The sky was incredible, sparkling, and the Milky Way was very clear. . pulsing group of stars in the western sky was flowing streams of bright light down to earth. I was there, with little rays of light shining down, pulsing on me from the West, saturating me with light and I felt suddenly uplifted. I was truly out of my body, ecstatic just being me, just being there. A feeling of peace and wonder filled me. The wonder of it made me pause right where I stood. I looked up and absorbed it all without question, happy. After an indeterminate length of time, I went back inside and fell asleep. Just like that.

Later that morning, the Lama explained he had been chanting for me and the young assistant, Thubten, translated what he said about my dreams and the Lama's prediction for me. I could never have imagined the magic of those words and the answers they gave me.

Before Thubten told me what the Lama perceived about my dreams, he told me a little about dreaming in general. Tubten said, "Many people dream about things in their immediate life first, going over things they are worried about or a problem they are trying to solve. Then others also continue dreaming and hit their past in this lifetime or in past lives—the lifetime after lifetime that the spirit lives through. A very few keep dreaming and dream about the future—things that are set in motion now, and will happen later. You have dreamed all three of these and saw present, past and future."

Then Thubten told me what the Lama said about my own three dreams. The first was about problems I was grappling with in the present: all the worry about if I should stay in Nepal, scenes of trekking, Simon, and thoughts about what I should be doing. The second dream was about past people and events, dipping into past lives that might have seemed vague, but to me felt true. And the third, the one with all the hands reaching towards me, was about my future. The Lama said it showed clearly what I should do and matched the perception he received during his nighttime chanting for me. He explained that he understood I would not be happy staying in Nepal as a monk chanting for years (*he got that right!*) but I needed to go back to America.

"*You will find your answers back home in the West,*" the Lama predicted. Thubten was sad when he recounted what the Lama said, as he cared about me and wished me to stay longer. But this was coming from the Lama, the top spiritual leader for thousands of Tibetan people in Nepal and other areas.

As soon as this prediction was said, I felt a shiver up my spine and knew I *had* seen the future unfolding. I instantly knew he was right. There are abilities and perceptions we have that we may never explore, but as an artist I always keep an open mind to the possibilities. *Well, it was a no-brainer!* My next move was to go back home to the West, and see where it would lead. I was suddenly certain and excited about what to do.

One of the dreams I remembered having as a little girl was slowly falling through space on my bed. I never hit anything nor did I hit bottom, I just endlessly floated there through dark endless space. It was what kept me from sleeping as a child. I thought I had to stay awake or something bad would happen. *Or something profound that I shouldn't miss,* I realize now.

Fear is a terrible debilitating emotion, keeping us from pursuing what we know deep down is right. I never imagined that my dreams were part of my own life, my own thoughts, hopes and decisions.

Just like that I was not scared anymore. My direction was clear.

Buddhist Stupa

Chapter Forty

Every Tourist's Nightmare

I NTENT ON GOING HOME, THE FIRST THING WAS TO GET A PLANE TICKET, but I needed money. I decided to go to the black market to exchange some of my currency int. Nepalese rupees. so I could buy the ticket—the banks would take forever.

The smell of the open air market—garam masala and more exotic Indian spices mixed with the smell of sweat and tobacco—and the noises of the market with screeches and squawks of animals from chickens to water buffalo, along with the human chatter in different languages, hit me right away. It was crowded with life. Trying my luck to cash in my currency on the black market to get more than I would at the local bank would mean I'd be able to go home. But, I guess I was too greedy or impatient and should have gone to the bank instead. I learned a big lesson that day.

As I walked among the stalls with copper bowls, spices, bolts of material, vegetables, jewelry and artifacts of Nepal, I felt a hand on my shoulder.

"Change money?" a stranger said to me while looking over my shoulder and glancing around us. That was my first clue. He was shifting his eyes back and forth like he was scanning the crowd, as we moved along the narrow space between the stalls. He was a younger, slightly built, dark Nepalese man. I was alarmed and he saw it in my eyes. "No worry, I get your money changed," he said to reassure me. He looked ordinary, a lot like any of the Nepalese in the city, with a small light patterned hat, cotton shorts and vest. Even though he was not that old, he had very old eyes and I wondered if he had a home or if he slept on the streets. I started to forget my fear.

"Yes, I need to change some money to get a flight home," I told him. "American, right?" he smiled at me with an indulgent look. *Do tourists all seem a little lame, lost, or out-of-it to the native population?* I thought to myself. Or maybe it was pride, showing his expertise to someone who had such a rich country. I wanted to trust him and it was getting late. I really didn't want to be here when it got dark.

"How much?" he asked. I had $500 in other money and needed to exchange it to buy the plane ticket. I opened my small money belt, strapped around my waist like a life line, and showed him the $500. He went quiet and put his hand out for the money. "You stay here, I know what to do. I go, come right back," he said. He was very calm and seemed to concentrate upon speaking confidently to me. I was hesitating and he saw it. "Must exchange before it closes. Not much time. Up to you," he told me.

When he patiently looked to me to decide, rather than push me into it, I felt better about it. I didn't realize he was thoroughly coached and trained to handle things with tourists so they went smoothly, without attracting unwanted attention.

"Okay, here, but I need it all at the best exchange rate you can get. I have to make my flight," I said as I tucked the money into his hand. He nodded and was off.

I never saw him again.

Waiting there for over an hour, I started walking around looking for him. But he had vanished, and with him all my money! I felt like the biggest fool on the planet. No one likes to be betrayed and it always makes you feel guilty somehow, like I should have known and been sharper, or not so trusting. Where I come from the people are known for their hospitality and kindness. It's actually called "Minnesota nice"—even if they are forcing it, they try to stay polite. But I was a world traveler now and should have known better.

Most people I met all over the world were genuinely interested and warm people, basically good. I got angry first with the thief and then with myself, as I made my way back to Hans George's house where I was staying. He was immediately concerned when I told him what happened and he called the police, who then said it would be impossible to find the thief. He could be miles away by now. Hans George knew the American ambassador who suggested he telex my parents for more funds. Well, that was my least favorite option, but it turned out to be the fastest solution.

Within a day I had my funds, wired from my mom via Western Union. I had a much greater appreciation for her at that moment, as she did not berate me for losing my money and was concerned about me. I was flush now, and ready to head back home.

I already checked on flights and as you can imagine the Nepalese airport was small, and I secured a ticket easily. The counter woman explained to me that I had to hop over to India first, and then catch a flight that stopped in Rome on its way to London. From London, I had a stop-over and could then catch another flight going directly to Toronto.

I started thinking of home and got a little excited. What would I discover when I returned? *The answers? My answer?* One thing I did know is that Simon was back home by now. I wanted to return and share my adventures with him. But first I had to say goodbye to my good friends in Nepal.

Chapter Forty-One

Goodbye to Kathmandu

HANS GEORGE WAVED TO ME ALONG WITH STEFAN AND THE REST OF the household. It was hardest to say goodbye to Harka, who had served as the house boy and everyone's charming friend. With a sly smile on his face he said mysteriously that he had "packed a going away surprise for me in my backpack."

I was curious, and as they called my plane and I was about to board, he whispered to me, "Lynda, I took metal frame of your backpack, cut open the tube, stuffed two pounds of very good hash in it, welded it shut so no one will find. You have happy time in Toronto and never forget Nepal!" *What?! I didn't want or need this and tried to think of how I could get rid of my backpack. Too late, they were boarding now!*

I practically jumped out of my skin when the ticket taker called my name. *Did she know?* As I boarded, I suddenly knew I would have that same frightening thought and nervously look around every time I boarded and debarked from planes, watching security men and guard dogs as I slowly passed by, thinking of what it would have been like as a Jew walking past Auschwitz thinking the Germans would grab you any second.

All the way through the trip I thought of it until I arrived in London. Never in my life had I known how excruciating it was to have to hold yourself back, knowing you were doing something wrong. That was a feeling I never ever wanted to feel again!

Leaving Nepal was jarring enough and now I had to worry about my backpack! I didn't really want to go, yet I was excited to find out what was in the West. *What was it I would find?* To relieve my stress, I started thinking of home and everything that had happened to me since I left.

I was returning home a lot more aware of the world around me, who I really was, and where I wanted to be, than when I left.

Chapter Forty-Two

Fire in the Bedroom

O N MY LAST TRIP TO ENGLAND, THE LONDONERS HAD TAKEN ME TO Stonehenge on summer solstice and we had camped out watching the sun come up hitting the stones, briefly spreading a rainbow of light around us. That was one incredible trip! I looked forward to seeing my companions again. I had been the American curiosity, and had made friends singing with David, the guitar player. I also got to know Jade, the head of the household, as well.

Being an American novelty and also a pretty, young girl, I was popular again as soon as I set foot in England the second time. It also didn't hurt that my Nepalese friend had stuffed hash throughout the metal tubing of my back pack. I was finally able to get someone to open it up and take a lot of it off my hands, as much as they could reach. I ended up giving away a lot of it to the London household (Freda and her boyfriend, two other couples, and Jade, the single guy).

The stop in London was a mistake, I realized later. But at the time, with the attention of at least two men who were courting me, and all of their friends smoking, drinking, laughing and playing music, I was caught up in the flurry of celebration, attention and admiration. That combination was a giant trap. While the guitarist, David, was playing, we kept looking over at each other and I could se. interest in his eyes. I liked him very much. There was definitely a spark there. He was good looking and knew it. I mentally held my breath to see what would happen next.

"Why don't you sing along with me," he said tuning his guitar. I was thrilled to contribute and sing along with his friends around me. You cannot imagine how your voice sounds to others until you see the reaction on their faces. Most people sound funny to themselves when they finally hear their own voice recorded. I am a soprano and learned to harmonize from my mother and sang in choir. Fortunately it was a positive reaction and I decided not to crawl somewhere and hide. David continued to play, as well as flirt with me, and when done playing, encouraged me to come upstairs for what I could imagine was some kissing and fooling around. I was lonesome from my travels, wanting a little passion from an admirer like him to feed the soul. So I was about to follow him up the stairs, but never saw Jade looking at us. (Later I found out from one of the girls that Jade had been eyeing me all night long and had a "crush" on me.)

When Jade came up the steps out of nowhere, I turned, and he starting talking to me. He was older and really the unannounced leader of the household, supposedly very smart. David moved aside for him and watched me for a minute then started downstairs. I was curious about Jade and admittedly a little flattered by the attention. *Was I feeling a bit stranded and lonely for male attention?*

Jade said, "I want to show you something," and indicated he wanted me to go upstairs with him to his third floor room. As I started going up the stairs, I remembered so clearly meeting Simon for the first time in London at the big futuristic furniture art exhibit and seeing him in the ceiling mirror. It filled me with the same strong sexual urgency that I had with Simon. I missed his touch so much I froze at the door with tears in my eyes. But an instant later I directed my attention to Jade, and decided I had to stay in the here and now. *Time to face facts; I may never see Simon again.*

We were up on the third floor room when David walked in. He started saying that he had a song for me, and brought his guitar out. The two men nodded briefly to each other, and I felt maybe it would be okay.

The room was large and filled with lighted candles, incense and a ton of old tapestries all over the walls. We all three started singing innocently to David's guitar. But it later turned amorous: we all threw off our clothes and ended up in one big bed. My shirt flew in one direction while men's pants flew in the opposite direction. The shoes were quickly thrown off with the rest of our clothes and the room looked more like a gaggle of teenagers had camped out here for a week, with no thought to the mess they created. One lone pair of undershorts ended up on a lamp stand, huddled against my bra which was hanging by a strap.

Our arms and legs were tangled together like a pretzel, trying to get a grip. Our kissing seemed to morph into giggles, and no one seemed to be able to do more with their privates than rub someone somewhere—or in the guys' case, try poking somewhere in the approximate area. We laughed so much when we did find the right place, often times someone moved and then switched positions s. we fell face down on someone else's rump!

Well, as you can imagine we were having a riotous time, but were completely out of it and drinking way too much English beer. We were trying to be so hip about it, being a threesome, but one of the guys (I think it was Jade) started to get a bit miffed.

Next thing I knew, someone (probably David) fell off the bed against a floor lamp, which knocked over some of the candles, which then lit the tapestries and the curtains on fire! *Chain reaction.* We had a fire which was starting to get out of hand!

"HELP! HELP! FIRE! THE ROOM'S ON FIRE!" I shouted along with the others. It was all hands putting out the fire and the whole household was awakened; everyone naked running around grabbing water and blankets to smother the fire until it was finally out. It looked a little like the silent films or bad ninja movies with everyone running around madly all at once. Almost comical if it hadn't been a real fire!

Boy, you can imagine how ashamed I was the next day standing at the doorway looking at a soot and water-soaked room that used to be Jade's. The room was still fairly intact and the rest of the house was fine, but I still felt guilty and responsible. David was there, and he was acting amazed that the room survived, as he looked over at me with a wink and smile on his face. *After all, it wasn't his room,* I thought, a little upset.

Jade came over to me. "It's not your fault, really," he quickly told me. "We were all to blame."

"But your room! I am sooo sorry!" I told him, giving him a hug.

"It'll be fine. We had some fun and a bit of excitement. Never did that before, so maybe it was worth it, don't you think?" he said quietly.

I hope Jade still feels fine about it when he has to sleep in it tonight! I thought.

Some of the others were laughing about it, but it's too easy to hurt someone's feelings or piss someone off if it's a threesome, and I thought it's not worth it to me. I learned a valuable lesson that day about men.

There was no way I could have predicted the disaster, as well as the final realization about men that I experienced. *It was my weakness, looking for love rather than creating it, got me into this trouble.*

Now I had to get back on a plane again and needed my backpack. Although Jade had welded it shut again so I could use it and disinfected it to take away any smell, I was aware it still had the remains of some hash inside. I'd not be able to get to it until I landed in the States.

I said "goodbye" to David, Jade, and the rest who saw me off with some relief, and I waited in line, worrying about several check points to get to my plane bound for Toronto. But they never said "boo," and I waltzed through all of them on my way through the London airport and boarded the plane, despite the terror I felt inside me.

Oh, no, I still have to make it through customs when I get to Canada!

Chapter Forty-Three

Going Home

MY FLIGHT FROM LONDON BACK TO TORONTO, CANADA, WAS IN THE evening. Going through the airport at Heathrow, in London, was hair-raising because of my backpack. But, I was finally on my way home! *Relief!*

Harka's hidden hash stuffed inside the metal tubes of my pack was weighing on my mind. As I approached the last customs officer, I felt my backpack growing heavier. My brow was sweating and I thought *this is it; they're going to pull me over and search me!*

I looked down at my shoes and remembered I was dressed casually, in my jeans and a shirt with a jacket, and not in my more hippie Indian skirt and blouse. Whew! I was glad I had washed out my American clothes and looked more the part of a girl on holiday. *Not a dope smuggling degenerate,* I thought as I suddenly realized that it was not part of my plan to be in this situation. Never again! "Miss, oh, miss!" the customs official said. I was startled when I looked over and my heart stopped. I kept thinking *he must know, he must know what I have inside my backpack. He's going to find it. I am totally screwed!*

"You forgot your passport," he said warmly. "You don't want to forget that now, do you?" he said.

"Oh!" was about all I was able to utter and scurried over to retrieve my passport from him. "Thanks a lot," I mumbled looking down, and felt like he could see right through me.

"May not wanna spend time lookin' for it instead of seein' the sights, now do you?" he said with a laugh.

I nodded "No" and flashed a smile. I was embarrassed, but had to go on.

He tipped an invisible hat in my direction and turned his attention to his next tourist. I stumbled off with my passport (and my backpack) toward the ladies' bathroom and went straight to the sink.

Running cold water, I splashed my face several times until I calmed down.

"Ah, you're one of those nervous fliers, huh?" I heard from an older woman beside me. "Well, you've nothing to worry about—unless you're some kind of criminal smuggling something on board," the lady said with a wink to show she was kidding, but I turned a little pale with shock.

"Come on, you should be just fine, really. Buck up your nerves now, the flight isn't all that bad," she said with a sympathetic tone to her voice.

If only she knew, I thought as I finally boarded my plane home, taking what seemed like forever to calm down and sleep. I started thinking about Harka. I suspected he got back some of the money I lost in the black market, with all his Nepalese connections. Maybe that was what he used to buy the hash to send with me. Perhaps he saw too many Americans trying to bring back hash from Nepal and thought I would like that, too. I brooded about this, exhausted after all my travels.

Falling asleep on a plane is tricky. Your head has to be at just the right angle or you tend to lean one way or another and wake up with a stiff neck. I always wondered why they couldn't have some kind of gel-padded seats to conform to your body and extend it far enough to hold your head, too. *Why not?* I'm certain the first airplane to install those kinds of seats would have so much business that all the other airlines would soon follow suit. Just imagine no stiff necks, no restless, uncomfortable, or testy passengers. Even the kids would settle down and sleep with nary an ear-piercing wail.

I often imagined inventions and things in the future, and even wrote some of them down to see if years from now they would actually happen. Realizing artists of all types tend to create things in more than one way, I remembered my mom telling me about the actors in the forties and even some now who were great singers and dancers as well as actors. This was called being a "triple threat" and sounded good to me!

Why limit creativity to only one thing?

My work would be waiting for me back at art college as well as all my friends. *And, Simon would be there*, I thought. The plane ride was my chance to wind down from my adventures, and I realized I really was tired. Time to snooze.

Chapter Forty-Four

Reverse Culture Shock

DESPITE MY DISCOMFORT AND EXCITEMENT I DID FINALLY SLEEP AND woke up with Toronto before me at night, spread out with millions of lights twinkling below us.

"Fasten your seat belts, we are about to land," came blaring from the speakers, and I caught my first sight of Lake Ontario and the huge city hugging its shores. I looked down at all the modern buildings, concrete, glass and steel, roadways, freeways and all the different kinds of cars below me looked so tiny and unreal. It seemed slightly sterile and a bit hectic with all the man-made structures piercing the landscape. I missed Nepal already and wanted to sit down with Harka over Tibetan tea. The feeling was so strong it was almost reverse culture shock. *Where were the mountains, hills, and rice paddies?*

My friends back in Toronto would not understand this, however, except for Simon. I caught a ride to my house from the airport from a friend who gave me the first welcoming kiss back. But even so, I immediately felt the difference when I stepped off the plane. *Was I the only one who was changed forever?* I thought as I ran into my house.

"Hey, let's get your bags and unpack," my girlfriend, Bridget, said and I followed along feeling a little numb. When we were unpacking, I had a sick feeling in my stomach and mentioned it, but my friend shrugged it off as jet lag, "that's normal, coming from a third world country like you did," she said with flourish. "Going half way around the world, and *all by yourself.* What were you thinking?"

"Ok, let me show you what I brought back," I told her a little defensively, and pulled out the Gurkha sword and silver earrings. That led to many stories and later I went out with friends who made me repeat the adventures I had in Nepal.

A few days later I received a package from Nepal. *A present?* It was from Harka and wrapped in very thick plastic. When I opened it, I found a neat pile of concentrated hash. *Oh, damn! Harka's at it again!* I looked out of my window thinking paranoid thoughts about officers storming into the house with guns raised! But no, there wasn't a knock on the door or some kind of hairy drug bust, so maybe I was safe.

Only thing to do was throw a party and give away or throw away all the hash. I didn't want it myself, and was definitely in the throes of reverse culture shock. *This city had none of the charm of Nepal that I missed so terribly.* But that never stopped me before. The good thing about the party is that Simon came over and we met up again for the first time since leaving Nepal.

"Hi! What's that?" Simon asked, pointing to my package.

"My friend Harka sent me a present from Nepal. I think he found out who stole my money in the Nepal black market before I left and may have gotten some of it back. From his experience, Westerners liked Nepalese hash which was worth more than money to some, so I suppose he thought he was doing me a favor. But, I'm not into drugs much anymore, even the primo kind," I said with a shy smile.

"Well, I'm surprised. You really did make many good friends over there, I hear. If you don't want it, I'll take some off your hands," he said with a wink.

It was bittersweet for me watching as he rolled a joint of hash in his careful manner and took a puff, like I had seen him do so many times in the several years we were together. We talked for a long time about what we both experienced in Nepal, and I realized how dependent I had been on him before Nepal.

The party was picking up as more friends arrived.

"You know, I always wondered why you came back to Nepal a second time," I said looking intently at Simon. The loud music was playing *Black Magic Woman* by Santana, in the background.

"I was interested in the people up in the villages when going to see Terry and Mary. They are so innocent, charming, living off the land. A simple life and I didn't get enough of it. I missed Nepal so much when I first got back to London I had to turn around and go back again," he said smiling. I heard *Samba Pa Ti* from the Santana album playing now and looked over at Simon. His expression was wistful for a second and then guarded. He abruptly changed the subject.

"Are you sure you don't want any of this?" Simon asked me. "Here, let me roll you a joint."

"No thanks, really," I told him as he looked at me with surprise. "The package was not my idea. I don't really like how the drugs make me feel. It actually gets in the way of my painting.. His expression was wary as he started taking out his cigarette rolling papers again and shrugged.

He never admitted that he also wanted to see how I was doing in Nepal. He had no idea what his friend Jay was up to in Nepal, either, and I wondered if he had tried to set me up with him. *I never noticed before how self-absorbed Simon was.*

I saw at once he had not made the same connection with the vast array of people that I had in my travels, and while he always had some interesting observations, I now felt there was something shallow in his experiences. Also I was holding back and reluctant to tell him much about my romances along with my travels since we broke up and felt it may hurt his feelings. Better to stay friends. Even though our recollections of Nepal were very different, we kept our friends entertained all that night with our stories.

He left with a big hug and kiss, and I was saddened by the finality of our relationship but still ever hopeful for the future. My own future this time and felt happier within myself and resolved to make it on my own.

Later the next day I felt a bit sick, and went in to see a doctor, a young intern, who told me after testing that I had amoebic dysentery. "It's common from tourists coming back from some Asian countries. Don't worry," he said.

Amoebas? Like little invisible cooties inside me? Wow! It must have been that water from the stream I was drinking from while trekking. I heard later that the water buffalos defecated in it. When the Nepalese drank from the water, they were probably immune, but obviously I was not! The strong anti-biotic he gave me did work, but made me sleep a lot.

I dreamed of being back in Nepal.

Chapter Forty-Five

The Visitation

A s healing processes go, mine was at the top of the list of "unusual" or even "extraordinary." I had to get out of the city, immediately, to see trees, grass, water—unencumbered landscapes. That weekend I went away to my friend Jasper's farm with a group of old friends. It was up north towards the Algonquin park area outside of Toronto and it had a lot of open space–green with golden farm land. Jasper was a very tall South African with blond hair, and I knew his girlfriend who told me "that was not all that was big on Jasper!" *Ha, ha!*

His farm house was large, with four or five bedrooms, and a big barn with a silo on the property. There was also a weather vane on the top of a twenty- foot tripod stand, spinning in the wind like an oversized pinwheel.

We were all running around, having some fun and Jasper climbed up the "windmill" trellis structure and announced when he got to the top, "*God is a woman, I just got the message and wanted to tell all of you,*" he shouted down to us.

The women nodded their heads in agreement and all the men laughed out loud. *Well why not? I thought. We're closest to godliness when we give birth, aren't we?*

It was here at the farm that I had an unexpected visitor that night in my room. The Lama, Tashi Gyaltsen, visited me as he had promised just before I left Nepal. He wanted to see what I was up to when I got back to the West. I was in the farm house, in the Algonquin park area, in my room at night. The last thought I had was that I had discovered something and would mail a letter to the Lama soon. I wanted him to see something I read and found and to tell him all about it.

It was very late and I was alone in my assigned bedroom. Tossing and turning in my bed, I kept thinking about so many things when all of a sudden I saw the Lama. He was sitting cross legged, right in front of me, just like I had seen him last. He came to me, a bit in front of me, off the ground, hovering in the semi-dark glowing in the moonlight. He just looked at me and smiled. *Yes, people can appear and disappear and project themselves if the will power is there. And some people can also see it.* As I learned in Nepal, there is magic in the world. I know how he made me feel just then and I gave him a greeting in thought only. The mental answer he gave me was strong, warm and reassuring. *Wow! I'm really perceiving this and it's good, not scary! I'm seeing him physically and spiritually and aware of his presence right here, right now, and it's okay. So cool!* He seemed ethereal and when he looked expectantly toward me, it was as if he was asking me how I was.

I am doing fine, but do miss Nepal so much. Tashi, I am finally over Simon and can stand on my own now. Also, I did find the answer to something else I was searching for a very long time, a way to get back to basic, to who I really am. Then I let him know what it was.

He looked over at me long and hard for a time, with a slight smile on his lips. We were both in a place where there seemed to be no time and no space—just us. And the thoughts, perceptions, kept racing between us very quickly.

Finally inspired, I thought, *I'll send you a letter and tell you all about it! I'll be fine...really,* meaning every word.

He nodded towards me and was gone. No trace of him. At first I thought it was just my imagination, but I was stone-cold sober and wide awake. I've heard about and read many stories about what the Lamas can do and how they can appear and project themselves. I know what I saw, felt, and heard. He was there, it was him.

Suddenly I remembered about my imaginary friend.

When I was two-years old my best friend was "Doo-but," who was invisible to others but plain as daylight to me—a benevolent spirit hanging around me. I talked to him, asked him things, laughed with him, got acknowledgements from him, relayed exciting things to him, even playing games with him. I had him as my companion for quite a while. Then, at four years old, my mom told me I would have to leave "Doo-but" home when I went to school, where I would meet lots of other kids my own age. I was disappointed. *Huh! Didn't she think other kids could see him, and would like him too?*

They never thought I was crazy, sometimes even to my mom it really did seem like there was someone else there, some kind of presence. They thought I had a big imagination and they saw that as normal, even artistic, and were tolerant of me.

But just before school started my mom told me, "Lynda, to other people Doo-but doesn't exist, and maybe no one else sees him but you." After that revelation Doo-but sadly told me he had to go now, and I rarely saw him after that.

Seeing the Lama appear before me, I remembered that special time so dear, with the entity that was around me as a child that perhaps only I could see, who protected me and played with me. I realized that was the time when I decided I had the ability to perceive what others may not. And that was okay.

More adventures followed when I returned to the West, just as the Lama had predicted. Now I could even tell the difference– those that saw and loved real magic in life and those who could only see or believe in material things. There was a *big difference* in what was valuable to people, and I would learn much more about it as life went on, but this realization was the first step, the biggest step.

Also, I finally fully trusted my instincts. For some people who scoff at imagination, the magic truly is gone. Imagination gives instinctive as well as reasoned-out solutions, using perceptions and your own creations of free will, of what you want for your own future. *You must really look at it, find the answers for yourself, and decide based upon what is the best for* all *concerned.*

Make the right choices, Layla. You will never regret them.

My vow was simple now—to keep using my imagination and never lose the magic I found in myself.

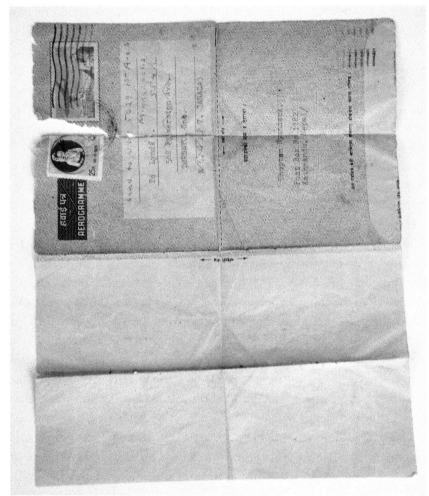

Letter from the Lama

Spiritual Nature of Love

F UNNY HOW YOU REMEMBER PEOPLE, LAYLA. SEE IF THIS RINGS TRUE FOR *you. I think you always continue to love someone you have loved in the past, even if in a different way. It's always about something good you first found in them, something that stays with you.*

I loved my very first boyfriend, Gary, beyond all limits, with the innocent passion of a fifteen-year-old. I thought we would always be together. With Simon, after finding him under unusual circumstances, I thought we were meant for each other. But it was never totally comfortable with him. With several men I met after that it was all about "they needed me" or "lusted after me" or "they loved me" so I had to be with them. I've learned that being in love with a man is a journey all by itself and a relationship has to be created almost daily.

Most women, if they really think about it, seek the experience of completely being loved as themselves, loved just as they are—including their faults as well as strengths. Also they want to completely see and know the other person in all his or her facets. If you can communicate and do that honestly, I think it can save relationships.

Along with embracing all aspects of a person, also comes the responsibility of helping them rid themselves of any negative influences, any unhappiness. Then we would not "need" each other as much as delight in the experiences of one another, whether as friends or in a shared life together—if fully open to it.

As for love of a child, after a difficult time in Duluth as a teenager, I promised myself that when I got married and had a family of my own, I would be the best mom ever to my kids, treat them as people, talk to them and always accept them no matter what they did. I was determined to keep an open mind and find a way to make things better for them, consult their understanding as well as help them reach their own goals. Kids flourish under that kind of parenting I think.

In general, I've always felt that I needed to do things that would make a positive difference in this life, or lift people up and make them happy, no matter what happens. Not just make myself happy, but help out others too—especially people who are open to it, really willing to perceive and learn.

How to make others happy? How to do that for the next generation—for my children, and for all our children's children? Naïve, you may say, but I have found this is a universal wish of all good-hearted mothers I've met everywhere.

Some things, like the feelings of love I refer to, are always with me, and you can look at those wonderful moments in your memory whenever you need to. They are there. And I have so many recollections of my exciting journey to Nepal to remind me life is an adventure.

As for my irrepressible optimism? The memory of those few years of bliss growing up "at the Lake" in Wisconsin remains the foundation of my eternal hopefulness. And every journey since then always, eventually brings me back home.

What did I really need to go through to reach higher states, peace of mind, or gain this happiness? Travel half way around the world to Nepal and back.

I grew up a lot, of course, while traveling and meeting different people. I was no longer the naïve child, no more oblivious of other cultures or people, and man-oh-man, was I able to stand up on my own and respond to dangerous moments! What happened to me on this journey changed how I viewed life and how I interacted with it. I became more uninhibited, not as confined to traditions, and much freer to make up my own mind, make my own decisions.

My journey gave me a direction in life, and the certainty that home was wherever I wanted it to be. Anyone who lives through rough times and comes out still hopeful and ready to build a future is blessed in more ways than they know. *"Building character" is what they call it. But, when you're in the grip of a depressing situation, things can look awfully shitty.* I saw that I could pull myself out of depression, without drugs. I could also fend off discouragement by *deciding* things would be all right. That year I had access to spiritual forces beyond myself, and found "me" in the process. With anything I wanted to do, I knew I just had to decide to do it, and do it.

At the end of this journey, did I find what I was I searching for? *Yes!* My pilgrimage was necessary to discovering the spiritual side of my own nature—that natural, intuitive, magical side that I believe is in all of us. My odyssey was needed in order for me to feel free to be myself in whatever I do in life so I can be truly successful at it. I learned that I did not want to be dependent upon others, men or women, to pull me through. But I also learned to be humble before the need for knowledge and gladly open to learning and enlightenment with the help of others. Mine just happened to be the Lama.

In that mystical place, Nepal, I discovered the answers to a great dream—to find out who I really am, spiritually, and what I am capable of. I used to think of myself as limited, that I had been only partially seeing things, caught up in various "it's only human" traps. Looking around, I didn't want to stay incomplete and restricted anymore, caught up in endless petty human troubles with few solutions. I needed to evolve into a new, bigger, more able self.

That's exactly the right time to draw upon the life force that motivates each and every one of us. *You know what I'm talking about.* Then just decide things will be all right and purposely work to make them that way. So, that's what I did.

And it worked.

What happened next is a story for yet another time.

Goodbye for now, my Layla. I wish you well on your own journey.

The End and Beginning!

Acknowledgements

It was Susan Stroh, writer's workshop leader extraordinaire and great friend, who first encouraged me to write my Nepal book. I have to thank her for sticking with me through this journey and making me confront and write everything that happened. Also I have to thank my great friends at the Claremont, California, writer's group— Lee, Peggy, Mary, and Karen who always encouraged me to continue and gave great feedback along the way.

My editor, Patricia Ross as well as George Gluchowski at Hugo House, both of them are invaluable and greatly appreciated. Cyndie Tobin did a great job as proofreader and also Ronda Taylor, the designer who took my own Nepal painting for the cover and made it into a window to my past. Great job all of you!

Finally I have to acknowledge all those who helped me in my travels until I finally found my own way. You know who you are and will always be remembered. Especially my great family, Anjuli and her husband Chris, Kelyn, my brothers, mom and dad and finally my granddaughter, Layla. My heart is always with you.

About the Author

BORN AND RAISED IN MINNESOTA AND WISCONSIN, artist, writer, and PR expert, Lynda Cain Hubbard, was spurred early in life by an urgent need to express her artistic talent and the love of the outdoors. She attended the Minneapolis College of Art, with a semester at the University of Minnesota. While at college, she taught art classes at a women's correctional institute. Her art has been displayed in galleries in California and Nevada and her paintings are on the wall in more than five states and Canada.

At twenty, she found herself heartbroken and bereft of a baby she gave up for adoption. She decided she needed to see the world, traveling from England, through Europe, Greece, and India, and finally climbing the Himalayas of Nepal. This gave her the chance to study different cultures, to paint and draw as well as to interact with the people—a story that she has finally put into print in Journey to Nepal.

To prepare for her trip, and while still in college, she did architectural drawings for a large Toronto firm. Upon returning from Nepal, she trained at a film studio, both on the set and in the marketing department. She moved on to advertising, PR (public relations) and trained in Internet marketing. She has been running her own marketing company, Trendsetters, since 1991, and her team conducts market research surveys in person as well as online. She has been writing copy and publishing articles for over twenty years, and keeps busy joint-venturing with consulting firms throughout the United States.

Helping literally hundreds of company owners, from small to larger companies and start-ups in their marketing and publicity, she decided to put all her experience down in a basic e-book and workbook on marketing for her clients. Know Before You Go: Marketing Basics for Any Business, which outlines what marketing really entails in a simple, no-nonsense approach. The companion workbook gives small and medium businesses excellent exercises and actions they can do to successfully market themselves in a competitive environment. She has appeared on college radio stations and has had articles on marketing and PR published online and in local newspapers in the Los Angeles area.

Her most cherished creation is a non-profit foundation for children's charities at: www.Hubleefoundation.org. The charity encourages new alternative energy sources as well as educational programs for children.

Ms. Hubbard currently lives in Southern California with her family, including a recently arrived granddaughter. You can visit her website at www.trendcreators.com. She welcomes constructive comments.

"The Art in each of us is the very best of what we are. Letting that come through in my own life is one of the best things I have ever done."
— Lynda C. Hubbard

www.ingramcontent.com/pod-product-compliance
Lightning Source LLC
LaVergne TN
LVHW022345060326
832902LV00022B/4261